Copyright © 1997 Jossey-Bass Inc., Publishers, 350 Sansome Street, San Francisco, California 94104.

Substantial discounts on bulk quantities of Jossey-Bass books are available to corporations, professional associations, and other organizations. For details and discount information, contact the special sales department at Jossey-Bass Inc., Publishers (415) 433–1740; Fax (800) 605–2665.

For sales outside the United States, please contact your local Simon & Schuster International Office.

 Manufactured in the United States of America on Lyons Falls Pathfinder Tradebook. This paper is acid-free and 100 percent totally chlorine-free.

Library of Congress Cataloging-in-Publication Data

Bunker, Barbara Benedict.
    Large group interventions : engaging the whole system for rapid change / Barbara Benedict Bunker, Billie T. Alban
       p. cm. — (The Jossey-Bass business & management series)
    Includes bibliographical references and index.
    ISBN 0-7879-0324-8
    1. Organizational change—Management.   2. Management—
Employee participation.   I. Alban, Billie, T.   II. Title.
III. Series.
    HD58.8.B86   1997
    658.4'06—dc20   96-26883

FIRST EDITION
HB Printing 10 9 8 7 6 5 4 3 2 1

The Jossey-Bass
Business & Management Series

For our grandchildren, all fifteen of them, and the
future of the organizations in which they will work and live

Contents

Foreword

Recently an associate and I facilitated a one-day meeting for about ninety people from a large nonprofit organization that produces educational and testing materials. They had been involved in a significant reengineering effort that was leading to a merging of two broad and significant functions. Now was the time to address organizational design and structure. How would the reengineering changes and the consequent merger affect the way they should now be organized and structured? The three top executives naturally wanted input from these ninety or so people, but more than that, they wanted commitment. They knew that without commitment no new structure would work. And they, as the top executives, had no intention of imposing a particular structure on their people. Following the principle that involvement leads to commitment, we designed and facilitated a day of activities that ensured involvement and contribution from everyone, that brought these activities to some degree of closure through small group presentations to the three top executives at the end of the day, and that developed a plan for implementation of the meeting outcomes during subsequent weeks.

My associate and I followed principles and practices that are presented in this book. Currently, these kinds of large-scale, high-involvement activities are more common than was true a decade ago. Moreover, the likelihood is that these types of organizational interventions will be even more common and prominent a decade from now. Why?

First, as Tom Peters warned us a few years ago, managers and leaders in organizations today want *speed*, faster responses and action steps to solve problems. They do not have the luxury of an intensive and comprehensive study of their organization that might require six months or so. They want action and they want it now. Yet the more sophisticated leaders and managers know that they cannot afford to sacrifice organization members' need to have a voice and a sense of ownership about changes that may be occurring in their businesses and institutions. The interventions and activities described in this book help to address the simultaneous need for speed and ownership.

Second, leaders and managers, at least the more astute ones, genuinely want ideas from their people. These individuals, who may be in positions of considerable power and influence in their organization, nevertheless know in the wee small hours of the night when they cannot sleep that they do not have all the answers. For a variety of reasons, organizational life today is too complex and too demanding for one person to have all the answers. Getting ideas from many people and getting them rapidly has therefore become a major driving force.

Finally, the fields of organization development and change management are starving for new social technology. Team building is not sufficient, and neither is a comprehensive organizational survey. These interventions continue to be useful, but today they, as well as other interventions that we have used for years, do not provide a totally satisfactory array of tools for our trade. We need new ideas and new social technology.

Interestingly, the basis for the social technology described in this book is not new. Many of the ideas and techniques described originated in the 1950s and 1960s. There are at least two differences now, however. One is that the large group interventions covered in this book are elaborations and extensions of and improvements on the earlier ideas and techniques. So what is presented by Bunker and Alban is new, yet based on fundamentals of group and intergroup dynamics that have been known for quite some time. The second difference is timing. Large group intervention is a social technology whose time has come. For reasons noted above, the timing for such interventions could not be better. Bunker and Alban have captured the moment—and expertly, I might add.

One additional point about the social technology that is involved in large group interventions is the combination of small and large groups and the "flow" or transitions between the two. This combination exists for all of the large group interventions described in this book. Small group work is more efficient and gives more opportunities for people to have a voice. Yet ultimate decisions, or at least recommendations for action or change, are usually made at the large group level. Understanding how to effectively conduct the shifts back and forth and the timing involved is critical to the success of these large meetings. Also, the small groups are usually self-directed, perhaps with recorder and facilitator assignments for a couple of group members, but no designated leader, and certainly not a formal one. The point is that we are only at the beginning stages of learning about self-directed groups and how to make them more effective. Large group interventions provide opportunities for us to learn a lot about self-directed small groups.

A final note: In a few days I will be leading a two-day retreat for a newly merged academic department. Although some of us know others in our new and larger department quite well, we do not really know the majority well. One of the first activities of this large group meeting will therefore be small group sessions in which we will get to know one another better. The primary question each of us will address and explain to our colleagues is "What do I feel passionate about in my work?"

It is abundantly clear that Barbara Bunker and Billie Alban are passionate about large group interventions. They have mined this field for several years now and have brought to us not only the ore from their mining but finished products as well. We are able to learn much from the two of them. Our learning comes easily because Barbara and Billie have not only done their homework; their additional gift is that they write about their subject with clarity and *feeling*.

Pelham, New York   W. Warner Burke
July 1996

Preface

Organizational life in America is currently in flux. Managers and consultants, working to improve organizational effectiveness, are searching for new ways to cope with the requirements created by the global market, changing economies, and the new expectations for both workers and companies. This means that organizations need to change in order to meet these challenges and to achieve quality and customer satisfaction.

This is a book for people who are looking for ways to bring about this change. In it, we describe twelve approaches currently being used by major corporations, nonprofit organizations, and communities to implement large-scale change and renewal. This is the first time that all these large-scale systems methods have been brought together in one volume.

What Is a Large Group Intervention?

Large group interventions for organizational and community change are methods for involving the whole system, internal and external, in the change process. These methods may go by different names (whole-system change, large-scale organizational change, the Conference Model®, Future Search, or Simu-Real), but the key similarity is that these methods deliberately involve a critical mass of the people affected by change, both inside the organization (employees and management) and outside it (suppliers and customers).

This whole-system change process allows a critical mass of people to participate in:

- Understanding the need for change
- Analyzing the current reality and deciding what needs to change
- Generating ideas about how to change existing processes
- Implementing and supporting change and making it work

For large group interventions to be effective, the issues addressed must be systemic; that is, they must affect a large number of people across all lines and levels of an organization. These methods have been used in change efforts concerning (1) changes in strategic direction, (2) acceptance and implementation of quality programs or redesign projects, (3) changes in relationships with customers and suppliers, and (4) changes in structures, policies, or procedures.

Why Use These Methods?

Two major problems with top-down change are the amount of resistance that it creates and the time it takes to put the change in place. Changes that cascade from the top often stagnate or get distorted. Even in situations where a representative group of employees is established to analyze a process and make recommendations for change, the effort takes time and the recommendations often have to be sold both to a management steering committee and to the larger organization.

Representative groups or steering committees that do not meaningfully engage key stakeholders do *not* produce commitment. Marv Weisbord (1987) is fond of saying that people will support what they help to create. When everyone is involved in the decision process, carrying it out happens faster and with less resistance.

It may seem strange, but getting everyone involved, even if it initially takes more time to plan and conduct change, is more efficient than trying to implement change "quickly and efficiently" using a small planning group. This is so because when everyone gets on board through these large group methods, less time is needed for implementation, and the implementation is more likely to be successful. One major advantage of these change methods is that it is not necessary to tell, resell, and finally beat the change into everyone. If an organization values ownership, commitment, alignment, and speed, it might consider using one of these large-scale, participative approaches.

Another advantage of using large-scale organizational change methods is access to information. The people who are closest to the problem or issue being discussed often have critical information that enriches the change strategy. However, because they also are often at the lower levels of the organization (or, in the case of customers, outside the organization), a traditional small group or top-down change strategy may not solicit their input. Large group interventions, by involving a critical mass of people, also access a critical mass of information that enriches the change strategy. In addition, with everyone in the room, organizations do not have to go out of the room to get information, so they cannot put off making change because "we need just a little more information."

A final advantage is that the diversity that comprises the whole system often creates a synergy that leads to more innovative change—a more creative solution—than a small group can possibly produce. This is the result of having a critical mass of people involved from the start.

How This Book Is Organized

This book is organized into five parts. Part One, the introduction, provides information on helping organizations deal with change in the 1990s, the development of large group methods, how we became involved with these methods of organizational change, and our ongoing journey as we learn and work with these various methods.

Part Two includes four chapters on methods that focus on developing a desired future: the Search Conference, Future Search, Real Time Strategic Change, and the Institute of Cultural Affairs (ICA) Strategic Planning Process. In three of these methods (the Search Conference, Future Search, and ICA Strategic Planning Process), participants co-create and decide on the vision of the organization's future or shape a specific issue in the organization's life. In the fourth, Real Time Strategic Change, the management proposes a strategic vision for the future, and the organization participates in shaping and ratifying it.

Part Three discusses four approaches to work design. The Conference Model®, Fast Cycle Full Participation Work Design, Real Time Work Design, and Participative Design are used to restructure or redesign organizations, usually after a new vision of the organization has been defined. Their key feature is their commitment to building full participation by involving significant numbers of people (stakeholders) in the restructure or redesign process.

Part Four covers four additional methods of whole-system participative work design: Simu-Real, Work-Out, Open Space Technology, and Large Scale Interactive Events. These methods do not propose creating a new future or direction; instead, they deal primarily with a plant or division's day-to-day issues. Their purpose is to surface work-related issues, especially cross-functional work tasks, policies, and procedures, and to discover ways to address these issues.

In the final part of the book, Part Five, we include a chapter on the dynamics of large groups. We discuss some of the innovations that are occurring in the field today. Then we focus on how companies can choose the method that is most appropriate for their organization or community and describe some of the guiding principles and values that underlie these large group methods.

For those with an interest in knowing more about a particular method, we have included an appendix at the end of the book that lists additional readings, videos, and training programs. Where possible, we describe how to contact these sources.

Acknowledgments

Over the past five years, we have spoken with hundreds of people whose experiences have enriched this book in countless ways. We want to especially acknowledge the people who have attended the three-day Large Group Interventions Workshop—which we have run several times each year since 1994—for the sustained dialogue that has developed from these experiences.

Among the delights of our work on this project have been the relationships that have developed with all our colleagues who have created these methods. We admire their work, but we admire even more their generosity of spirit. They have supported our poking around in their backyards, they have invited us to come and watch them work or work with them, they have listened to us talk about them, and now, they have read what we are saying about them! Without the spirit of learning and inquiry that they all share, this could not have happened.

Our work has been forwarded in many ways by Tom Chase, who began by helping us to organize our first public seminar and who has become a center of information about Large Group Interventions and the moving force in creating the Large Group Interventions Case Conference in Dallas, Texas.

We want to especially thank Marcelene Anderson, Dick Axelrod, Emily Axelrod, Warner Burke, Steve Cabana, Chris Cappy, Laura Christenson, Ralph Copeman, Co-Vision (San Francisco), Marlene Daniel, Kathleen Dannemiller, June Delano, Susan Dupre, Sue Eichorn, Fred Emery, Merrelyn Emery, Rick Everett, Barbara Feldman, Al Fitz, Walter Grady, Elaine Granata, Gary Hochman, Harvey Hornstein, Harry Hudson, Robert Jacobs, Beth Jandernoa,

Sandra Janoff, Lawrence Jimiken, Fay Kandarian, Steve Kerr, Donald Klein, Don Krebs, Kathleen Leahy, Terry Lombardi, Sr., Bridget McCarthy, Frank McKeown, Metasystems (Washington, D.C.), Douglas Meyer, Ashok Nayak, Harrison Owen, Bill Pasmore, Carol Pasmore, Chuck Phillips, Don Pomraning, Ernesto Poza, Bob Rehm, Sam Salter, Fred Smith, Laura Spencer, Kate Stechem, Noel Tichy, Paul Tolchinsky, Cathy Tolchinsky, Chief George Wapachee, Marvin Weisbord, and Gil Williams.

Special acknowledgment goes to Clay Alderfer, editor of *The Journal of Applied Behavioral Science*, for supporting our vision of a special issue on large group interventions in 1992, before this was an established area of change practice; to our editors, Byron Schneider, Cedric Crocker, Mary Garrett, Helen Hyams, and Bill Hicks, at Jossey-Bass; to Beth Richards for her editorial help; and to Douglas Bunker for his interest and support, not just of this book's evolution but of our constant phone calls and trips in pursuit of understanding and clarification of this practice arena. We wish to thank Barbara's colleagues in the Portsmouth Consulting Group, on whom some of the early ideas were tested and whose enthusiastic response emboldened her. Undoubtedly, we have not mentioned some people who should have been included. We regret and are accountable for any omissions.

Finally, we want to thank each other. One of the great pleasures of life is working close in on a cutting-edge project with someone whom you like and who complements and augments your own capacity. We know how rare such an experience is and we treasure it.

Buffalo, New York   Barbara Benedict Bunker
Brookfield, Connecticut   Billie T. Alban
July 1996

The Authors

Barbara Benedict Bunker is a social and organizational psychologist who has worked for the past twenty-six years as a professor in the Department of Psychology at the State University of New York (SUNY) at Buffalo. At SUNY she has been, at various times, head of the Social Psychology Doctoral Program and director of graduate studies and has trained many students in organizational psychology and consultation.

Bunker began her professional life with a graduate degree (D.B., 1956) from the Divinity School of the University of Chicago; she then worked for eight years as Director of Religious Life for the Woman's College at Duke University. In the course of providing leadership training for Duke students, she discovered social psychology, specifically the field of small group research and practice. This led to a new career direction and more graduate education, this time in social psychology.

She returned to New York City to complete her Ph.D. degree (1970) in social psychology at Columbia University. While at Columbia, she worked with Matthew Miles, Ron Lippitt, and Goodwin Watson on some of the earliest organization development (OD) projects in school systems. She met Billie Alban at early organization development meetings in the New York City area, and the two have been good professional colleagues and friends since then.

Bunker's interest in the application of social psychology to organizational issues has been expressed in her writing about organizational change processes, small and large group dynamics, gender in work organizations, theory of practice, commuting couples, and trust in work relationships. She is the author of numerous articles and books on these topics, including *Social Intervention* (1971, with H. Hornstein and others), *Mutual Criticism* (1975, with M. Levine), and *Conflict, Cooperation, and Justice* (1995, with J. Z. Rubin).

She is an internationally known organizational consultant to a variety of clients. She has taught in executive development programs at Columbia, Pepperdine, and Harvard Universities and is often invited to present at national conferences on change. She served for seven years on the board of directors of NTL Institute in Washington, D.C., including three years as chairperson. In 1984 and 1991, she held Fulbright Lectureships in Japan, first at Keio University and later at Kobe University.

In addition to her very full professional life, Bunker enjoys the quiet of her new house by the brook on the family farm and planning for her next international junket.

Billie T. Alban is a nationally recognized organizational consultant and organization development practitioner whose career spans four decades. Her clients have included a broad range of Fortune 500 companies, including airlines and companies in the financial and manufacturing sectors. Her work with multinational companies has taken her to Europe, Asia, and Latin America.

She began her professional life by pursuing a career in the theater, graduating from Yale with a Master of Fine Arts degree. Shortly after graduation, she married and went to live in Ecuador, where she taught drama at the University of Guayaquil and started a repertory theater group. As her two small daughters grew up, she became active in helping her husband manage the family marine transportation business, where she confronted a number of the situations described in this book and first did large group work (without knowing that was what she was doing!).

After fifteen years overseas, she moved back to the city of her birth, New York, where she worked in the Poverty Program as a community organizer. She has always had a strong interest in involving people in creating their own future. As the field of organization development emerged, she established her own consulting practice. She was one of the early staff members of the NTL Program for Specialists in Organizational Development. Over the years, she has been an important mentor in the lives of many developing OD practitioners, teaching on the faculty of programs offered by UCLA and Pepperdine and Columbia Universities.

Alban served for many years on the National Board of the Organization Development Network. She also served a term on the Board of Governors of the American Society for Training and Development and received the Lippitt Award for excellence in the field of organization development.

In 1992, she and Barbara Bunker edited a special issue of the *Journal of Applied Behavioral Science* on large group interventions, in which, for the first time, examples of different methods of large group intervention were presented together as an area of practice. In addition to her work with Bunker as a formulator and educator in the area of the practice of large group interventions, she has an active pro bono practice in her own community, Danbury, Connecticut, where she has been working with the city on issues of violence using large group methods.

In the midst of this busy and rewarding professional life, Alban loves fishing with her two granddaughters in her boat on the lake in Connecticut where she lives.

Large Group Interventions

Part One

An Introduction to Large Group Interventions

Chapter One

Of Mud Flats and Solid Brass

Sometimes stories from our past are prescient of our future. We begin with the story of a very threatening emergency in my (Billie's) husband's family business. It shows how at times, without knowing what we are doing, we know intuitively what to do. In this case, it was a decision to involve the whole system in solving the problem.

The business we were in was marine petroleum transportation in Ecuador. We got word from the Ecuadorian Navy that they had received an SOS from one of our tankers. The tanker was adrift in the Pacific and had radioed its coordinates. It could not have happened at a worse time; it was the middle of Carnival, just before Lent, when all our employees were celebrating in one extended party and I was the only family member in town. But gradually we were able to round up the crew, serve them some coffee while they sobered up, and get them off on a tugboat to look for the disabled ship. They found the ship and towed it back to Guayaquil, Ecuador, in a few days. But that was only the beginning of the problems. We were a small firm. We only had three tankers, and every day of interrupted service meant the loss of a great deal of money.

The problem was quickly diagnosed. The main drive shaft that goes from the engine to the propeller had seized up, probably from some dirt in the oil used to lubricate it. Normally, it would have to be removed from the ship and turned on a lathe. The nearest dry dock that would hold the tanker was in Panama, so I called to find out whether, if we towed it there, they could supply us with a dry dock and do the repair. My heart sank when I heard that they had no openings for three weeks, and then it would take another month to do the repair. It was doubtful that the business could sustain this kind of delay and loss. What to do? I explored several possibilities but each led to a dead end. Finally, I was out of ideas and getting desperate, so I decided to discuss the situation with my employees.

We had a small but loyal group of workers, consisting of the captain and sailors, the shore crew, workers in the machine shop, and the repair staff. I called a meeting and asked everyone to come. I also invited our customers, the Anglo-Ecuadorian Company and Esso, as well as representatives from the Ecuadorian Navy, who had helped to train the crews. About forty people were present as I laid out the situation and told them everything I knew, including our financial limitations. I also had to tell them that if we could not get the ship back in working order, we might not be able to meet our payroll. Even if it had been possible to do the repair in Panama, the cost of towing and repair would have been too great, in both time and money.

I asked the group if they could figure out what to do. I served coffee and food and they crowded together in small groups to discuss the problem. It was loud and chaotic; people were drawing pictures on the tablecloths and waving their arms. Finally, late in the evening, out of what seemed like total chaos, the captain announced loudly, "Señora, we've got a solution!"

Their solution was inventive and very risky. They wanted to tow the tanker up one of the narrow estuaries at high tide (there were no dry docks large enough for our ship in Guayaquil). As the tide receded, it would beach the ship in the mud flats. Tankers are flat-bottomed, so there would be no risk to the ship. They would then have between four and six hours to remove the shaft. This involved taking the propeller off, removing the stern bearing, getting the shaft out and onto land, and replacing the stern bearing and propeller so that when the tide rose, the ship would be sealed again and could be towed to a safe anchorage. Then the shaft would be taken to our machine shop, where the land-based maintenance crew said that they thought they could turn the shaft by hand in about two weeks. There was no lathe in town that could turn a shaft of this size. (Turning the shaft is an exceedingly meticulous process. The shaft is shaved and measured in micrometers. It must be exact to the micrometer across the whole length of the shaft, from the engine to the propeller.)

I was facing two very risky procedures. One question was whether the crews could get the shaft out in the time they had. The other was whether the machine shop could turn it by hand to the prescribed tolerances. (Our insurance agent from Lloyds of London was very pessimistic on this latter point and strongly advised against trying it.) But being inexperienced, and without other options, I decided to gamble. We would try their plan!

The next day we towed the tanker up a narrow estuary. This was difficult work, most of it in the mud. I hired two bands to play music and stationed them on opposite banks of the estuary. They would alternate with each other to play and keep everyone's spirits up. Families came and helped with the food and liquids I had ordered for breaks. The big flatbed truck that would take the shaft to the machine shop was stationed nearby. We were all excited and concentrated intensely on the task we had to do. The captain was in charge of removing the shaft; everyone worked feverishly. When the shaft was out, the head machinist would take over and supervise loading it onto the truck. Four and one half hours later, just as the tide was beginning to come in and make work impossible, we breathed a collective sigh of relief. The shaft was out and the ship was sealed. We were jubilant!

For the next two weeks, our attention focused on what was going on at the machine shop. We all would drop by to lend support and see how the work was going. Would our people be able to do this exacting work? I hoped desperately that they would, but the pessimism of the agent from Lloyds made me anxious.

The day came when the delegation from the machine shop appeared at my door and said, "It's ready!" I called the inspector from Lloyds, who came down from Panama with his assistant to pass judgment. He frowned deeply and shook his head as he moved down the shaft, measuring it every inch along the way. The shaft glistened in the morning sun as my foreboding deepened. Finally, as we waited in silence, he reached the end, looked up, and pronounced his verdict. "Perfecto!" he said with obvious amazement and smiled. A great shout went up. It was a moment that I shall never forget. For years, I have carried that image with me as a reminder of what can be.

Only later in my career as an organizational consultant did I have the theory to explain what happened. Now, I know that I was dealing with a complex systems problem. As the management, I did not have the answers to the dilemma, but I knew that the people closest to the problem had a great deal of intelligence, and I engaged them in solving it with me. I gave them all the information that I had to work with and facilitated their work in any way I could think of. I also got the significant stakeholders involved with us in solving the problem. We were fully aligned as an organization around our goals. I wanted to preserve the company, our employees wanted to preserve their jobs, and the stakeholders wanted to continue in business with us. Together we took risks and turned a potential disaster into a win-win solution. That is what this book is about. It is about new methods that are currently being created to get the whole system involved, knowledgeable, aligned around a set of goals, and moving in concerted action.

It is common knowledge that organizations at every level are feeling pressures to change. Businesses need to become more productive, customer-focused, and global. Schools need to educate better while at the same time dealing with the problems that students bring to school with them. Community agencies need to develop collaborative coordination strategies. Arts organizations are struggling to survive funding cuts. Few organizations escape these pressures. At the same time, the nature of jobs and of work is changing, at least in the United States. Employees are working longer and harder, and it is no longer the case that managers know more about the work than those they supervise. People need to be better educated to get good jobs.

Many writers have called attention to the difficulty that hierarchical and bureaucratic organizations have as they try to deal with the changing environment. Cutting out layers of middle management may make organizations flatter, but it has not made them more flexible, nor has it made their employees more involved in and committed to organizational success. The truth is that we live in uncertain times. No formula exists for global success. If a right answer exists, it is unknown. Organizations are trying to find ways to be responsive to new situations, to position themselves in the face of these uncertainties.

Although management clearly has the leadership role in taking action, in today's complex work environment they seldom have all the answers. Figuring out what is going on and what we ought to do is not the same kind of task that it was in a more predictable world. Everything seems to be changing at the same time, and old forms of analysis are no longer useful in predicting the future. Confronted with this situation, management has several choices. One is to continue in the old paradigm, to act even if they do not know what they are doing and hope for the best. Unfortunately, we have been in some companies where this appears to be what is happening. This maintains the hierarchy and the illusion that someone is minding the store.

Another choice is to create a new way of working that is more collaborative and democratic and that does not rely on the small top group for all the answers. Organizations that are going in this direction have an underlying assumption that their people possess great talent and creativity that is untapped. They propose to create a new relationship with them for everyone's benefit.

I (Barbara) ran into a wonderful example of such a paradigm shift the other day when I scheduled my graduate class in group dynamics to visit a team-based organization in Buffalo, New York. We arranged a visit to Outokempu American Brass Company and the

United Steelworkers of America, Local 593, to find out how their teams were working. During our visit, we discovered that this plant had a terrible labor-management history in the 1970s and 1980s. They had strikes every three years for twenty-one years. The only question was how long the strike would be this time. Then, in the mid 1980s, when most of the other brass companies in the United States were going belly up, a group of local investors decided to buy the troubled plant, but on the condition that labor and management had to change their relationships and collaborate if the company was going to survive.

Over the last ten years, the new organization and the union have completely turned themselves around. When we talked to workers from the machine shop or press department, they talked like owners. They understand the business environment, they understand and talk with their customers, and they know what it means to put quality and customer satisfaction first. In other words, they are now putting all the energy that used to go into fighting each other into survival and figuring out how to be the best in the business. Management holds them accountable for results. They hold management accountable for providing resources, monitoring the environment, and allowing them to do their work. These people like coming to work. They feel challenged and they feel successful.

Workplaces like these are characterized by high involvement and shared decision making, a de-emphasis on status, a shift from the command-and-control modality to discussion and working through differences and conflict. Everyone depends on everyone else. This is the climate in which it makes sense to talk about "learning organizations" (Senge, 1990). As Argyris (1982) has pointed out, learning can only occur when people are committed to examining assumptions and are open to feedback. In contemporary organizations, it takes everyone's knowledge to solve complex problems and create the flow of information needed to come to good decisions. In the methods described in this book, the whole system gathers to do this kind of inquiry. The assumption is that a great deal of information is already within the organization and can be made accessible. Involving stakeholders in these events makes even more information available.

Not only is this a new social innovation, but it is changing the nature of the practice of organization development and of organizational change. Although notions of participation and involvement underlie the whole history of organization development, traditional practice using survey feedback methods has had the consultant collecting information from the system and then summarizing it and feeding it back for discussion and action to improve system functioning (see Table 1.1). For the most part, the change was initiated within the organization itself, sponsored by the senior management. Often, the process began there and slowly cascaded down the organization. By the time the lower levels heard about the data, the information was often months old.

Table 1.1. Organization Development Strategies for System-Wide Change.

	Traditional Data Collection and Feedback Methods	Whole-System Interactive Events
Theory Base	Action research	Open systems theory
Purpose	Improved organizational effectiveness	Alignment around a strategic direction, work redesign, system-wide issues
Data Base		
• Source	• Internal to organization	• Organization and external stakeholders
• Availability	• Limited to units	• Widely shared
Responsibility and Accountability	Driven by senior management	Broadly shared by senior management with whole system
Time	Slow: Waterfall process by level	Fast: Rapid response to data
Learning About:	Individual or unit functioning	The organization as a system
Consultant Role	Central to: • Data collection • Data interpretation • Data feedback process	Structures and facilitates: • Data collection • Data analysis • Action taking
Change Potential	Sequential incremental change	Simultaneous fundamental change

In the new paradigm, the whole system gathers to create and analyze its own data. Often, outside stakeholders who represent important information and relationships are included in the process. Because the organization is well represented in the room, decisions and actions happen rapidly, with little waiting around. Everyone is there; thus the results do not have to be sold to the rest of the organization and simultaneous fundamental change can occur.

The consultant's role is different in this new paradigm. Rather than gathering, summarizing, and feeding back data, a process that makes the consultant very central, the consultant's role in large-scale events is to create structures that enable systems to collect and analyze their own data and make their own decisions. Large group interventions begin as events, but, as you will see, they can become new ways of managing in complex times. They require of management a willingness to democratize the workplace; they are not techniques for getting people to go along. They are genuinely participatory. They hold great promise for dealing with the uncertainties of the world we now face.

Chapter Two

A Brief History of Large Group Interventions

Large group interventions emerged at the confluence of three intellectual traditions: social psychology, psychoanalytic theory, and systems theory as applied to organizations. Once in a while, we run into consultants doing large group events who do not seem to know anything about the intellectual history or development of the interventions they are leading. We believe that an appreciation of the theory that underlies the emergence of large group events is critical to the appropriate use of these events. This chapter is our description of how these three strands of theoretical thinking created large group interventions with organizational systems.

The Lewinian Tradition

A quick look at Figure 2.1 shows the three strands of development. We have focused only on the main contributors, so we do not present this schema as exhaustive. Readers are invited to consider other scholars and practitioners whose work they would include.

Gestalt psychology, which emphasized the holistic configuration of psychological events as contrasted with atomistic theories, developed in Germany early in this century and came to the United States in the late 1930s, as World War II was beginning, in the person of Kurt Lewin. Lewin fled the Nazi horror and was deeply concerned with the relevance of psychology to social problems; his Field Theory (Lewin, 1951) was based on physics and emphasized human behavior as the product of a dynamic field of forces. Lewin's work created the new discipline of experimental social psychology.

Figure 2.1. History of Large Group Interventions.

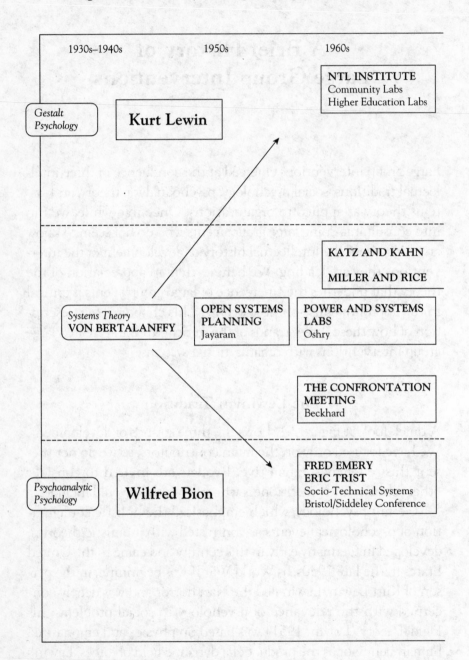

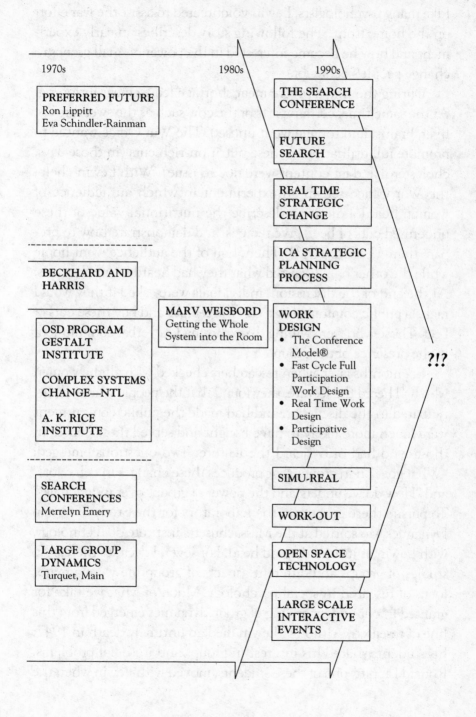

1970s   1980s   1990s

PREFERRED FUTURE
Ron Lippitt
Eva Schindler-Rainman

THE SEARCH CONFERENCE

FUTURE SEARCH

REAL TIME STRATEGIC CHANGE

BECKHARD AND HARRIS

ICA STRATEGIC PLANNING PROCESS

OSD PROGRAM GESTALT INSTITUTE

COMPLEX SYSTEMS CHANGE—NTL

A. K. RICE INSTITUTE

MARV WEISBORD
Getting the Whole System into the Room

WORK DESIGN
- The Conference Model®
- Fast Cycle Full Participation Work Design
- Real Time Work Design
- Participative Design

?!?

SEARCH CONFERENCES
Merrelyn Emery

SIMU-REAL

WORK-OUT

LARGE GROUP DYNAMICS
Turquet, Main

OPEN SPACE TECHNOLOGY

LARGE SCALE INTERACTIVE EVENTS

Like many psychologists, Lewin volunteered to assist the war effort on the home front. The following story describes an early experiment and how he became interested in the power of small groups to change people's behavior.

During the war, a severe meat shortage led to meat rationing. At the same time, certain parts of the cow such as the sweetbreads, liver, brains, and tongue went unused. The War Office wanted to promote full utilization of these nutrition-rich cuts (in those days, cholesterol and fat content were not an issue). With Lewin's help, the War Office set up an experiment in which an audience of women heard a dietitian describe the nutritional value of these underused cuts of beef, give recipes, and demonstrate how to prepare them (Lewin, 1943). Then, half of the audience went home while the other half discussed what they had heard in small groups. At the end of the discussion, individuals were asked if they would make a public commitment to try the recipes and buy these cuts of beef. Those who were willing to do this made a verbal commitment in the presence of the group.

Six months later, when researchers checked with all the women who had heard the lecture, they found that the people who had participated in the discussion and had made the public commitment were much more likely to have bought and served these cuts than those who had only heard the lecture. Two questions emerged: "What goes on in groups that produces these changes in behavior?" and "How do we understand the power of groups over individuals?" To pursue these questions, the Laboratory for the Study of Group Dynamics was started at the Massachusetts Institute of Technology, with Lewin as its founder and head. For several decades thereafter, studies of groups and different aspects of group life were a major focus of research in social psychology. Much of what we take for granted in our understanding of group dynamics emerged from this line of research. Although Lewin died an untimely death in 1947, his students shared his interest in groups and in social problems. Ronald Lippitt, one of these students, moved with Lewin when the

Center for Group Dynamics was established at the University of Michigan. It later became the Institute for Social Research.

Lewin's interest in social change involved him and Lippitt with adult educator Leland Bradford and psychologist Kenneth Benne of Boston University in a project on race relations in 1946. They collaborated in planning and running a two-week training conference for community leaders on race relations in Connecticut (Marrow, 1969). During the conference, participants met in discussion groups that were observed by Lewin's students. The researchers met every evening to discuss their observations from that day and to develop theories about group process. The story goes that a few conference participants grew interested in these evening research discussions, appeared one evening, and asked to attend. Lewin agreed and the first discussion was so fascinating that more and more people began to attend, talking about and reflecting on their own experiences in the discussion groups.

This process of being part of a group and then reflecting on the process of that group gave birth to a new social innovation, what is commonly know as the "T group" or sensitivity training group. Building on this discovery, Bradford, Benne, and Lippitt founded the National Training Laboratories (now the NTL Institute), an organization dedicated to helping people learn about groups and about themselves as members and leaders of groups. During the 1950s and 1960s, the NTL summer campus in Bethel, Maine, was a hotbed of experimentation in experiential learning. Businesses, churches, educational institutions, and communities were all interested in how T groups and experiential education could help them reach their goals. Even though this was a time of intense learning about small groups, the training setting, a two-week "laboratory," sometimes contained large groups of 100 or more. Although much of the time was spent in small groups, the laboratory also met for community sessions and experiential activities in which the training staff learned about designing for the dynamics and processes of very large groups.

Knowledge about small group functioning and design skills for planning experiential learning events are the basic skills used by the creators of several of these large group interventions. Real Time Strategic Change and the ICA Strategic Planning Process, for example, developed directly from this tradition, and Future Search incorporates training designs from the tradition. Many of the consultants who are practicing work redesign have NTL training and experience as part of their background.

In addition to group dynamics, university researchers studied task functioning in groups—how decisions were made, problems solved, and actions planned and implemented. As it became clear during the 1960s that T-group training in organizations was not effective, the focus turned to problem solving and fixing the deficits in organizational functioning that could be identified. The method of choice was survey feedback, an action research method that collects data about how the people in an organization view the organization and the functioning of their unit and other units. It is used to identify sources of ineffectiveness so that attention can be paid to remedying the situation. Consultants collect and analyze data and feed these data back to units that then take action to deal with the issues.

Ron Lippitt, like other organizational consultants of his time, engaged in this process with organizations. As a researcher, however, he also studied the process. While listening to some tapes of problem-solving groups at work, he realized that their discussion caused him to lose energy and feel drained and tired. Since problem solving seemed to drain energy, perhaps he could find something that would engage people in a different way and thus generate energy. Ron Lippitt was a creative genius at designing processes. He began to think about how past-oriented problem solving is. It looks at what has happened and tries to fix it. What if you asked people to think about the future? What if you asked them what kind of future state they would like to have in their organization? Lippitt (1980, 1983) began to create activities that helped people to think their way into a "preferred future." We remember some of his early experiments with groups at NTL's Bethel campus, where we were all asked to imagine ourselves on magic carpets five years in the future, hovering over our organizations and looking down to see what wonderful things were going on. Lippitt's experiments with the preferred future confirmed what he had suspected, that thinking about what you want creates energy in people. He began to work in this area in organizations but, even more important, he began to work with large community systems like cities.

The 1970s were a time when the automobile industry was in decline in Michigan. Lippitt and his colleague, Eva Schindler-Rainman, got involved with a number of cities across the country, but especially in Michigan, helping city leaders to bring together people from all parts of the community in order to think about and plan for the future of their city (Schindler-Rainman and Lippitt, 1980). Lippitt even created a system of voting with computer cards that allowed large groups of people to register their views. Then he immediately displayed the tally to the whole group. In some settings, Lippitt brought together as many as one thousand people, with remarkable results.

Although many other consultants knew about the work that Lippitt and Schindler-Rainman were doing, they were not quick to adopt it. Only recently has the field looked back and acknowledged how visionary and ahead of its time this work was. Lippitt and Schindler-Rainman trained hundred of consultants in preferred-future technology during the late 1970s and early 1980s in their NTL workshops at Bethel. Kathleen Dannemiller, who was Lippitt's student, took over these workshops when he became ill in the mid 1980s and developed her own work on large-scale events from this base.

The Tavistock Tradition

Parallel developments occurred in the United Kingdom, but from a different theoretical base than in the Lewinian tradition (see

Figure 2.1). The Tavistock Institute in London, England, was created to make social science knowledge applicable to individual, group, and system issues. Wilfred Bion, a psychiatrist and psychoanalyst associated with the Institute, found himself unable to treat his caseload of returning veterans from World War II because the numbers were too great. He decided to experiment with psychotherapy in groups rather than individually. His initial view was that he would treat each person in front of the others and that might possibly have a positive effect on the observers. What he soon discovered was that a great deal more went on in groups than simply his interaction with the patient. The group itself had dynamics that could assist or sabotage the task; it even could attack and undermine him as the leader. He began to think and build a theory about what he was experiencing. Eventually, he wrote a book, *Experiences in Groups* (1961), in which he described three basic assumptions that can either facilitate or inhibit the primary task of the group: dependence, fight or flight, and pairing.

The Tavistock Institute began providing training in group processes using Bion's framework in 1957. These ideas were carried to the United States in the person of A. K. Rice, who began running conferences to train professionals in identifying and understanding group processes in work organizations. The A. K. Rice Institute and its network of regional associations (see Appendix) make training available in this theoretical approach. Their training explores issues in small groups, intergroup dynamics, and the dynamics of large groups or systems. A large group is a group that is too big for face-to-face interaction, typically thirty or larger. The Tavistock approach has developed theory about the dynamics, issues, and dilemmas of participation in large groups (Main, 1975; Turquet, 1975). We believe that these understandings comprise crucial knowledge for practitioners who choose to work in groups that are too large for face-to-face interaction; we will discuss them in Chapter Fourteen.

Another central figure in the developments in Britain was Eric Trist, who, with Harold Bridger and Wilfred Bion, was one of the founders of the Tavistock Institute. Trist was a colleague of Bion in action research during the Second World War and an admirer of Lewin's work. Trist and his young colleague, Fred Emery, developed the idea of Socio-Technical Systems from studies they did in the British coal mines in the 1950s (Trist, Higgin, Murray, and Pollock, 1963). They developed a process for analyzing and achieving the best fit of social and technical systems in organizations that has been widely used in Europe, especially in Scandinavia, since the 1960s.

In the course of various consultations with industry, Trist and Emery were invited to help design a conference for the top leadership of Bristol/Siddeley, a recent merger of two aeronautical engineering companies. The organization's leader had in mind a leadership conference with invited speakers, but Emery and Trist had something different in mind. In their work at the Tavistock Institute, they had been studying the adjustment of industry to turbulent times, and they proposed a week-long exploration of the business environment, the aeronautics industry, and the desirable future role for Bristol/Siddeley; this was a clear departure from traditional organizational events. A compromise was achieved by preserving the days for the search process suggested by Trist and Emery and the late afternoons and evenings for speakers and discussion.

The week contained its points of stress and strain, but by the end, the group was talking like one company and had "redefined the business they were in" (Weisbord, 1992, p. 30). This was the first Search Conference (Trist and Emery, 1960). It was a dialogue among the participants that began with trying to understand the external world and then moved through explorations of the industry to their own company. The goal was a strategic action plan about the future. Emery took this experience with him when he returned to Australia, where he and his wife Merellyn developed the Search Conference method. Merellyn Emery has taught and refined the Search Conference over a thirty-year period in Australia and around the world.

Systems Theory

The third stream in the development of large group interventions is the enormous impact that open systems theory has had on thought about organizations. Including the organization's environment as a key element in understanding organizational functioning was a paradigm shift. Understanding that changes in one part of the system affect the whole was another. Eric Trist credits Fred Emery with bringing the implications of Ludwig von Bertalanffy's thinking about biology (von Bertalanffy, 1950) into the Tavistock Institute. Emery was clearly one of the earliest to grasp the implications of systems theory and to use it in thinking about organizations as open systems. Later, colleagues Eric Miller and A. K. Rice (1967) published their book on organizations as open systems. In America, at the University of Michigan, social psychologists David Katz and Robert Kahn (1978) published the first edition of their now-classic open systems approach to organizations in 1966. But even though these ideas were in print, they were only gradually moved into the practice of organizational change.

One of the early published designs for working with the whole system in the room was Richard Beckhard's Confrontation Meeting, published later in the *Harvard Business Review* (Beckhard and Harris, 1967). Beckhard invented the Confrontation Meeting out of a desire to shift the negative energy in a family business he was working with to a positive direction. This one-day intervention begins with heterogeneous groupings in which people consider what would need to change for life at work to be better. In other words, it begins with future possibilities. After the results are shared and organized, functional groups meet to develop four or five "promises," actions they can take in the direction of a better work environment. At the same time, they select a few priorities for management attention. At the end of the day, these actions and requests are shared and management responds. A two-hour follow-up meeting in about six weeks helps to sustain the changes and create others. This is the first design we know of that worked with all parts of the organization at the same time. It is not surprising that it emerged at the same time as Beckhard's work on complex systems change.

Training programs for consultants with open systems thinking at the core were started by the Gestalt Institute of Cleveland, Ohio, and the NTL Institute in the early 1970s. The A. K. Rice Institute also offered training in small, large, and intergroup dynamics from a systems perspective. Beckhard and Harris's book on complex systems change was published in 1977. Developments outside the field of organizational change also had an impact, for example, Jayaram's open systems planning model (1977) had wide effects on strategic planning and change in organizations. At a more experiential level, Barry Oshry (1996) developed a simulation in the mid 1970s called "The Power Lab," which allowed participants to explore the dynamics of being at the bottom, middle, or top of any system. People who came to these three-day events lived in their assigned role and enacted and studied the system dynamics in a large group.

The 1980s

The 1980s were a time when the field of organization development matured, or at least many of the senior practitioners in the field now had twenty years of experience. They had come through the eras of survey feedback, team building, and other strategies for organizational improvement. Working with executives of major corporations, they came face to face with some of the limitations of improvement-oriented change processes. A lot of talk was heard about "transformational change," a new kind of change that would alter the whole organization at once rather than following the slower waterfall-type process that was characteristic of earlier technologies. But few intervention strategies were commensurate with the talk of transformation.

One of these senior practitioners, Marvin Weisbord, who was well known for his thoughtfulness about his own practice, used writing a book about the state of the field of organization development to reflect on his own extensive experiences working with organizations and to rethink the history of management practice in the United States. *Productive Workplaces* (1987) examined in a new light the contributions of Frederick Taylor, Douglas McGregor, Eric Trist, Fred Emery, and Kurt Lewin to the way that organizations are run and changed. This reframing of management history was interlaced with Weisbord's own new practice theory.

One part of this new theory stressed the importance of "getting the whole system into the room" in order to create effective change. Drawing from all three traditions (see Figure 2.1), Weisbord created the Future Search as a method to get the whole system to decide on its purposes. He believed that stakeholders outside the organization could contribute to rethinking what was needed in the fast-changing world of new customer requirements and new technology.

Weisbord's thinking struck a deep chord with many of us. It resonated with our own experience and frustrations. The notion of getting the whole system into the room was congruent with our experiences when we had worked to make change only to have it all come undone because of changes in other parts of the system. It felt like an idea whose time had come.

Other influences also affect the methods we describe but are difficult to fit into the three streams of influence. The work of W. Edwards Deming (1992), for example, and the Total Quality Management movement have focused attention on what customers inside and outside the organization need and want. It has made it not only acceptable but critical to include stakeholders. Quality circles and Total Quality training have given currency to increased participation in problem solving for all organization members and to the idea that knowledge and good ideas are available at all organizational levels.

Twelve Methods for Getting the Whole System into the Room

As we turn to the 1990s and the twelve methods shown in the last column of Figure 2.1, it is now a great deal easier to talk about the ideas and assumptions that influenced these methods.

The two different forms of Search Conference originated in the Tavistock tradition with the Emery Search Conference. Weisbord and Janoff's Future Search was influenced heavily by the work of the Emerys and Eric Trist, but it has been modified by the Lewininan-NTL tradition.

Real Time Strategic Change and Large Scale Interactive Events (Dannemiller and Jacobs, 1992) come directly from the Lewinian-NTL tradition. The same is true for the ICA Strategic Planning Process and for Simu-Real. Work-Out also benefited from this tradition as well as being quite similar to Beckhard's Confrontation Meeting.

The four types of organizational redesign all came from Trist and Emery's original Socio-Technical Systems design, but each has been expanded to include large group events and participation by the whole system as well as by stakeholders. Participative Design is the next iteration of Fred Emery's commitment to democratic workplaces. According to recent statements by Emery (1995), it corrects some of the flaws in Socio-Technical Systems design and allows workers to truly control and be responsible for their own work.

Open Space Technology is difficult to categorize in terms of its theoretical roots. It was developed in the context of interest in organizational transformation. Harrison Owen (1992), who created it, has both NTL and analytic training. Rather than proceeding through a series of carefully orchestrated, structured experiences, participants in Open Space are challenged to find within themselves issues of deep importance and are invited to join others and discuss them. The agenda that the participants create makes possible the opening of whatever creative or emergent patterns there might be. Because no one knows in advance what they will be, the participants should be "prepared to be surprised." Theoretically, this seems close to the work of David Bohm (1990) and the work that is currently going on at MIT around the Dialogue Process, which emphasizes asking exploratory questions and examining assumptions and inferences (Senge, 1990). It is a nonlinear way of making progress under the assumption that deep structures can emerge if we allow them to. It is also the case, however, that psychoanalytic theory like Bion's may be very helpful in understanding the large group dynamics that occur, especially to the facilitator whose job it is to "hold the space"—that is, to maintain the integrity of the structure and process.

All of these methods of working in large groups are highly participatory. They fundamentally assume that people want to be engaged and to have a voice. But Open Space Technology assumes, to a greater degree than the other interventions, that people are capable of structuring their reality and of organizing themselves for the tasks at hand—and that being responsible for the events as well as the content will be energizing and lead to innovation.

Our Contribution to the Field of Large Group Interventions

We still remember our excitement and the conversation when it all started. As core faculty members of the Columbia University Advanced Program in Organization Development and Human Resources Management, we were spending three weeks a year together; this resulted in many interesting sidebar conversations about the state of the art in organizational change. One evening, as we were sharing information with each other about what people we knew in the field of organization development were doing, we were suddenly struck by a common pattern that we had not noticed before.

Barbara: Hey! Do you realize that even though these big events are very different in outcomes, they're also very different from the traditional practice of organizational change?

Billie: Yes, all of them seem to be working with very large groups of people who represent or are the whole system.

Barbara: And there's none of the one-to-ten or two-to-twenty staffing ratio that's so typical of team building and other kinds of interventions.

Billie: And it's so fast! None of the trickle-down waterfall sort
of work with the organization that takes forever. They're
all there in one room and they make decisions on the spot!

Barbara: Do you suppose it's possible that we're seeing some kind
of new social innovation, like the invention of sensitivity
training in the 1960s?

Billie: It really does feel like a breakthrough, as though something
quite new and different is emerging in practice.

Barbara: Someone needs to pull it all together and make sense
of what's going on. If this is really a paradigm shift in organizational change practice, people aren't seeing it that way.
They're just noticing interesting little aberrations on the
landscape here and there.

Billie: Why don't we do it? Why don't we try to make sense of it
and see where it takes us?

And we did.

What seems very clear now was quite murky back in 1991 and
1992 when we first began to notice and consider what was going on.
Marvin Weisbord's book, *Productive Workplaces* (1987), had a profound effect on us. Getting the whole system into the room made
sense; it felt right. And it probably was said at a moment in history
when we were ready to listen. It certainly gave us permission to
think differently about organizational change.

About the same time as our Columbia conversation, Clay
Alderfer was just assuming the editorship of the *Journal of Applied
Behavioral Science*. He let his colleagues know that he was ready to
create a change in format and was open to proposals for special
issues. We decided that a good way for us to think about what we
saw going on would be to propose a special issue on large group
interventions (Bunker and Alban, 1992). Clay was receptive, and
we went to work. We issued a call for papers because we were clear
that we wanted to know about any and all work that was being
done. We also talked with colleagues who we knew were doing
large group events and solicited articles from them.

Our thinking also progressed as we developed presentations for the national meeting of organization development professionals, the Organization Development Network, in 1993, 1994, 1995, and 1996. Initially, we could identify six different methods of doing work in large groups for the purpose of systems change. As our thinking and the field have developed, we now find that we can identify twelve methods in three outcome groupings. We often invited our colleagues who are doing the work to these sessions to "hear us talk about what they do." To our delight, many accepted, came to the sessions, made their own comments, and stayed to talk further with other colleagues about their work. At that point, we began to realize that we provided a context in which people who could think of themselves as competitors could stand easy and talk with other practitioners. We saw then that what we were really up to was providing a conceptual overview or cognitive map of these new ways of changing organizations. We were not trying to sell any one method; our role was to think and to educate. We could therefore bring people together to discuss developments that none of us fully understood. It was wonderfully exciting and had overtones of the atmosphere that had existed in the 1960s when most practitioners were university faculty with norms of sharing data and inventions and learning together about effective change practice.

In 1994, we began to offer public workshops on the topic. The people who came were usually experienced practitioners who were quite knowledgeable about the field. Our thinking continued to develop as we talked with them and learned about their practice. In this context, we began to test out an idea. Initially, we saw these events as very interesting large-scale meetings, events that had powerful effects on the organizational or community system. More recently, we see evidence in some organizations that large-scale events have become a new way of managing the organization and getting things done.

In 1995, Tom Chase of Conference Support Systems (a meeting management firm in Northwood, New Hampshire) proposed and sponsored a very successful conference in Dallas, Texas, on large group interventions with the Organization Development Network that presented cases by teams representing different roles in the change process from organizations that had used large group methods. We served as the anchors and commentators for the conference, which appears to be well on its way to becoming an annual event.

When our special issue of the *Journal of Applied Behavioral Science* went into its fourth printing and exceeded four thousand copies sold, we decided that it was time to write our own book. In this process, our thinking has again advanced. We have gotten clearer about ways to compare the methods and organize them, and we have attended more of these events and done more work ourselves. We think that these events require different skills and competencies of practitioners, although they are built on a base of traditional ones, and also require a different role in relation to clients. They hold more possibilities than we have thus far realized. We are writing this book to share our ideas with you and to invite you to join us in thinking about this new form of practice.

Don Klein recently commented about our work, "I'm not sure whether Barbara and Billie are documenting a movement or creating it!" We think the answer is "Both!"

On what to read next: If you are the kind of person who prefers to read all the theoretical material before you read about applications, you will want to turn to Chapter Fourteen and read the material on large group dynamics after reading this chapter. If, on the other hand, you like to get right into the central content, the description of each method, no detours are necessary. Read on.

Part Two

The Methods

Creating the Future Together

In the early 1970s, Billie attended a "life planning" workshop. At one point in the workshop, participants were asked to envision a day in the life of their ideal future and to describe what they were doing, the types of activities they were engaged in, and the people they were working with. Ten years later, while cleaning out a desk drawer, Billie came across the life planning folder. To her amazement, all but one of these future scenarios had come into being. (She never did learn to play the guitar!)

The same thing happens to corporations and communities when they "plan their lives." A clear, focused vision of the future has a magnetic power, pulling companies toward that which they picture.

Cascading the Change

In organizations, the traditional approach to change and new direction has been a process in which a senior executive team recognizes the need for change, then decides on the new direction and the changes required to implement it. The executive group then cascades the changes down throughout the organization, hoping that they will be implemented without too much resistance. Often, even middle management has little understanding of the "why" of these changes, nor is there a clear picture of their direction or vision. Employees traditionally are not included in these upper-level deliberations, although their contributions might be valuable and their commitment is essential for the change's success. External stakeholders (customers, suppliers, funding sources) are also not included, although they might bring valuable insights to support the change or to help the company to avoid creating a change that has a negative impact on a customer or supplier.

Over the last few years, creating a *vision* for the organization's future has also become popular. These methods have been promulgated by books on leadership, by leadership training programs, and by work done by the consulting firm, Innovation Associates, including Peter Senge and Robert Fritz (Fritz, 1989). Nothing is wrong with creating a vision. Unfortunately, the process used by corporate executives and their teams to write the statement of the company's vision and values often uses the same "cascade" approach noted above. Even when management talks about "enrolling" the rest of the organization in the vision or, as Senge says, the "shared vision"—involving the rest of the organization in this process rather than resorting to selling or coercion—the results are often disappointing. The key questions are: How do you create a shared vision? And what would happen if the whole system actually *participated* in creating the organization's vision and values?

This part presents four methods that help organizations to create their desired future vision and develop action plans for achieving the vision (see Part Two Figure). These methods are: the Search Conference (Emery), Future Search (Weisbord and Janoff), Real Time Strategic Change (Dannemiller), and the Institute of Cultural Affairs (ICA) Strategic Planning Process.

Part Two Figure. Comparison: Large Group Methods for Creating the Future.

THE SEARCH CONFERENCE
Purpose: To Create a Future Vision
Merrelyn and Fred Emery

- Set Format: Environmental Scan, History, Present, Future
- Criteria for Participants: Within System Boundary
- Theory: Participative Democracy
- Search for Common Ground
- Rationalize Conflict
- No Experts
- Total Community Discussion
- 2.5-Day Minimum
- 35 to 40+ Participants
- Larger Groups = Multisearch Conference
- 1/3 Total Time Is Action Planning

FUTURE SEARCH
Purpose: To Create a Future Vision
Weisbord and Janoff

- Set Format: Past, Present, Future, Action Planning
- Stakeholder Participation, No Experts
- Minimizes Differences
- Search for Common Ground
- Self-Managed Small Groups
- 18 Hours over 3 Days
- 40 to 80+ Participants
- Larger Groups = Multisearch Conference

REAL TIME STRATEGIC CHANGE
Purpose: To Create a Preferred Future with System-Wide Action Planning
Dannemiller and Jacobs

- Format Custom-Designed to Issue
- Highly Structured and Organized
- Theory: Beckhard Change Model
- Common Data Base
- 2 to 3 Days + Follow-Up Events
- Use of Outside Experts as Appropriate
- Use of Small Groups and Total Community
- Self-Managed Small Groups
- 100 to 2,400 Participants
- Logistics Competence Critical
- Daily Participant Feedback
- Planning Committee and Consultants Design Events

ICA STRATEGIC PLANNING PROCESS
Purpose: Strategic Planning

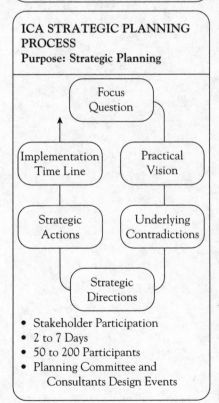

- Stakeholder Participation
- 2 to 7 Days
- 50 to 200 Participants
- Planning Committee and Consultants Design Events

Chapter Three

The Search Conference

Several months ago we received an excited phone call from a friend who had participated in a Search Conference in Crestone, Colorado, where our friend had bought some property. This small town was rapidly growing as people fleeing urban congestion and the "condominiumizing" of the ski areas moved there, seeking to build community in a more pristine wilderness area.

The people who had recently moved to the area, and those who already lived there, became alarmed over the damage that unmanaged growth could potentially cause. A very diverse group of residents felt a strong need to explore together what they wanted for their community. Over 150 people attended the Search Conference, which was structured as a "multisearch" with three groups of 50 people each, running in parallel. Following is our friend's report on the conference.

As I arrived at the potluck supper that initiated the conference, I was astonished at the diversity in this small community. We had writers, political leaders, environmentalists, developers, and businesspeople. How could we ever find common ground? We started the evening by forming a large circle. People told stories about the history of the community and events that stood out for them in terms of what this community is about. It was a wonderful start; I left feeling proud that I am part of the community.

The incredible thing that happened on the second day was that we discovered the values we shared. We analyzed the turbulent external global environment as well as the things that affected our community right now. The pivotal point for me came when we created a picture of what we ideally wanted for our community. Not only was there agreement among the 50 people in our room, but the lists from the parallel groups in the other rooms were almost identical to ours. We then met as a total group, all 150 of us, to go over the goals. We ended with eight strategic goals, including such things as sustainable agriculture, sustainable architecture, a new self-governance structure, infrastructure issues (water, roads, sewers), and the social infrastructure (education and health). Then we each signed up to work on a strategic-goal task force.

What amazes me is the follow-through from these action planning groups. After three months, we held an "all action group" meeting. All the action groups came together to report on what they had done, what they were planning to do, and what help they needed. People from the larger community who had not attended the Search Conference were also invited. Two new action groups were formed at this meeting, one to look at the needs of young people in our community and another to explore the need for a new post office.

Each month our local newspaper reports on the activities of each action group. This keeps everyone informed. Now, six months later, things are moving along; the agricultural group has formed a seed bank, the wilderness group has mapped some wilderness areas, and another group has been working on a new governance system that will include town meetings and allow for more true citizen participation.

The Search Conference is a participative planning method that enables communities, institutions, and organizations to identify, plan, and implement their most desired future. It was created in 1959 in England by Fred Emery, an Australian, and Eric Trist, an Englishman, to design the successful Bristol/Siddeley merger mentioned in Chapter Two. As we have indicated, Emery and Trist were both members of the Tavistock Institute in London and were influenced by the theoretical work of Wilfred Bion, also a member of the

Tavistock Institute. Fred Emery and his wife, Merrelyn, eventually returned to Australia, where Merrelyn Emery continued to develop the Search Conference as a method. She has now worked with these methods for at least thirty years and is currently training people in the United States in both Search Conference and Participative Design. Of the different approaches we will examine in this book, this is one of the best tested, with a very explicit theory behind it (Emery and Purser, 1996).

Steps in a Search Conference

The attendees at a Search Conference are selected on the basis of their expertise, knowledge of the system, influence in the system, and ability to implement outcomes. In addition, before the conference, everyone is thoroughly briefed and has an accurate sense of what he or she will be doing. The conference usually has from thirty-five to forty people. (Recent conferences in the United States have had as many as sixty people.) When increased attendance is needed, multisearch conferences are held, either in parallel or sequentially. Multisearch conferences require integration of the data that emerge from each conference; thus, more coordination and management are necessary. The design has six basic steps.

Discussion of Our Turbulent Environment

Environmental scanning is key to the Emery approach. The theory is that we need to be proactive toward environmental change rather than just reactive. This is accomplished by the following process.

As a total community, people call out their perceptions of the significant changes that have occurred over the past five to seven years; these are recorded on flip charts. All perceptions are valid—everything goes up on flip charts.

In small task-force groups, people analyze the data and develop both probable and desirable futures going forward a few years.

Common ideals for the future emerge from this session, for example, respect for differences, nonviolent ways of resolving international conflict, and a better balance of work and family life. These lists are reported and integrated and become the guiding principles for later work.

At times the Search Conference may do a similar scan of the environment that directly surrounds the issue under discussion. For example, a group may examine the trends and major issues affecting their division at that moment, ranging, for example, from loss of market share to new governmental requirements for waste disposal.

Our System's History

In this session on "where we come from," the total community, in an oral, storytelling session, describes critical events and changes in the existing system that have occurred over time. A wall chart is often used to record data. With the longer-term employees speaking first, participants describe what was happening when they joined the company and talk about the key issues and events they recall.

Analysis of Our Current System

The total community brainstorms the features or characteristics in the current system that need to be kept, dropped, or created in order to improve the system. Again, all perceptions are valid.

The Most Desirable System

People break into small groups that work in parallel on this task. The groups come up with a list of the key elements that describe the system they would like to see at a given point in the future. The groups then report and integrate the data. The entire community decides which futures should be developed into strategic goals.

Action Planning

At this point, participants select the strategic goals they want to work on and form self-managing teams to develop action plans for their selected strategic goal. The theory of managing constraints is briefly discussed to highlight the importance of listing constraints and developing tactics other than direct confrontation to deal with those obstacles.

The action planning groups develop the next steps, intermediate goals, time frames, responsibilities, and a method for coordinating and monitoring progress. At some interim point during this planning period, the work in progress is shared with the community. This provides an opportunity for feedback and a reality check showing that the work that is being done will serve the interests of the whole community.

Then, each group presents a final report to the total community. Follow-up is planned by the whole community (not the consultant or conference managers) and usually includes what the report will be, who should do it, and by when; to whom the report will go; and when to meet again.

Implementation

A unique feature of the Search Conference approach is how very explicitly this method deals with implementation. The assumption is that people do not need experts to implement action plans for them; instead they have the ability to make sense of the world around them and can create their own future. Thus, the Search Conference process sets up a highly democratic, self-managing community. As people move to implement action plans back at the workplace, it is important that the work not be co-opted into hierarchical, bureaucratic structures. Commitments are often made at the end of the conference to keep the self-managing structure, but in some traditional organizations, the "new" ways of working together may be overwhelmed by the "old" structures that are already solidly in place. These bureaucratic structures may have departmentalism, information systems, reward systems, or policies and procedures that get in the way of the work flow and discourage the cross-functional relationships that may be key to effective output or productivity.

One option Merrelyn Emery offers to help reinforce the new culture is to include Participative Design (see Chapter Ten) in the implementation phase, to create a democratic self-managing work organization in the workplace or in the community.

The Search Conference in a Corporate Setting

At the beginning of this chapter we included an example of how this method worked for a small community. Following is an example, reported by Douglas Meyer and Walt Grady at the Large Group Interventions Conference in Dallas, Texas, in 1995, of how a Search Conference was used in a corporate setting, at a division of the Hewlett-Packard Company.

> The Search Conference was conducted in the manufacturing division to develop future strategies and included the top three levels of management as well as cross-functional representation from within the division. The conference's stated purposes were to build a shared understanding of the internal and external environments in which people had been working, to create a future to which they could all commit, to begin action planning, to build a communication plan, and to ensure broad responsibility and commitment to implementation by involving others in the process. This division also desired to become a model of operational excellence within the company and to increase its leadership position within the industry.
>
> Before the Search Conference began, organizers collected feedback and data about how the other divisions perceived this one, as well as about some of the important changes that were going on in other divisions that might have an impact on the manufacturing division. At the start of the conference, participants shared their purposes and hoped-for outcomes. In small groups, they discussed

their expectations. After these reports were shared, participants put a picture of a large globe on the wall, and the total community called out the changes going on in the world that were important to their future. Items mentioned included global competitiveness, the entry of new competitors into the marketplace, and the tremendous pressure to reduce costs.

After looking at the global trends that affected their business, participants, in small groups, discussed the probable future if trends and business were to continue as they were at the present. Participants asked themselves what their most desirable future was, or, if they did everything "right," what their corporation would look like in the year 2005.

Next, the participants moved to their immediate surroundings and looked at what was happening in their company's and division's business environment. This included items such as a shortage of silicon, the problems caused by managing an increasing number of suppliers, and the impact on their division of expanding operations to the Far East, tariff policies, and the weakening dollar.

Participants then formed a huge circle to talk about history. The "elders" of the organization spoke first, recalling milestones, turning points, and key events in the division's history that stood out for them. They named events such as their excitement when the division was being founded, the close relationships between employees, and the fact that in the early days there were few security issues (although someone remembered that a bomb threat had once occurred). As the relating of the history progressed, a number of people noted, with some sadness, how the necessary increase in security had changed the makeup of the company as well as how some of the values of the founder had been modified or even lost as the company grew and changed. They also discussed the turmoil that business growth had engendered—having to absorb more and more people and dealing with the difficulties that this absorption and adjustment presented.

In the next phase of the Search Conference, the participants brainstormed, as a total group, what they wanted to keep, drop, and create. Using three flip charts with three people writing, the group called out their views on these three categories. All ideas were accepted and written down. The participants noted that some of the key ideas related back to the division's history—the old values and ways of doing things—and that the emerging ideas related to keeping these values, dropping a lot of the security and power plays, creating standardized core processes, and developing core competencies.

Next, the participants left the past and moved into the future. In this step, given the data that they produced and shared, participants worked in small groups to generate their most desirable future by the year 2005. Each small group generated six outcomes, encouraging one another to "dream big" while also being as practical as possible. The ideas generated by the groups were then placed on the walls, gallery-style, and everyone moved through the gallery to look at all the ideas. One person from each small group stood by the sheet and briefly reported on the desirable futures devised by that group.

In small groups, participants then developed criteria for selecting the top five strategies for achieving the future. One of these strategies was to improve two core business processes. The participants looked at their lists of ideas and chose the ones that fit under the chosen criteria. During this process, similar ideas were combined and any items about which people disagreed and that could not be resolved were placed on a separate "disagree" list to be dealt with at a different time. It is essential in this process that participants move ahead only on strategies that they can all agree on.

People were then asked to form new small groups, choosing which strategies or outcomes they wanted to work with. In these self-selected groups, people could rewrite or reword their strategies. Next, they listed some of the constraints they thought they might encounter in moving toward a particular strategy. The key task of this section was to find a way around constraints—for example, objections to costs or disagreement about marketing strategies—to achieve a goal. It is essential that participants not try to deal with these constraints earlier in the process, because doing so will restrain their creative thinking. By the time they reach this point, however, they are ready to develop tactics to deal with the constraints.

After dealing with the constraints, the groups reported their strategies and tactics to the whole community, receiving feedback from the community as they proceeded. The action groups then developed plans to accomplish the outcome, with short- and long-term goals, resources required, and time lines. Again, these plans were shared with the total community. The final step was developing a plan for communicating the ideas, involving others, and getting commitment from the larger organization.

Some of the unique features of the Search Conference are how it deals with the system in the context of its environment, its emphasis on a community of people taking action to make their desirable future happen, and its strong oral culture. Consultants experienced in using this method say that the task of the conference manager is to suggest conversations that are worth having: about systems history, what can be learned from the changing environment, and what the participants can accomplish together.

Because of its focus on achieving this shared future vision, its commitment to recognizing and analyzing the strengths and weaknesses of its current system, and its emphasis on achieving implementation through action planning, the Search Conference has proved to be highly successful for this division of Hewlett-Packard. In particular, it has been effective at aligning the division with the larger business goals of the organization and improving the core business processes.

The next chapter discusses another future-oriented method, Future Search. At the end of Chapter Four, we will look at both the Search Conference and Future Search, examining their strengths as well as exploring their similarities and differences.

Chapter Four

Future Search

As mentioned in Chapter Two, Marvin Weisbord drew on systems theory and on the work of Eric Trist, Fred Emery, Merrelyn Emery, and Ronald Lippitt, as well as on his own considerable experience, to create the Future Search Conference that he and Sandra Janoff are currently teaching, applying, and refining. Probably the best known of all the whole-system, large group methods, Future Search has been publicized in Weisbord's *Productive Workplaces* (1987) and *Discovering Common Ground* (1992), and in Weisbord and Janoff's *Future Search* (1995). Training programs now exist that educate people who are interested in using this approach, and SearchNet, an organization of Future Search Conference practitioners, has also been formed.

The purpose of the Future Search Conference is to explore possible agreements between people with divergent views and interests and to do consensus planning with them. It brings together at one time and, literally, in the same room, everyone who has an interest in the issue to be discussed. It is future-oriented, helping organizations and communities to agree on what they want and on their future goals. The Future Search Conference is a planning strategy that is especially suited for complex systems issues, including dilemmas within an organization, an educational system, the community, or the environment. For example, it has been used in companies to explore issues connected with their future, in school systems to investigate site-based management, and in a community in California to address housing issues. The process allows people to explore what is happening in the larger environment, understand the need for change, co-create the future together, and formulate action plans.

Future Search Conferences are highly participative; they involve those who can contribute to the issue or have a stake in it and are built on the strong belief that people will support what they help to create. This is in sharp contrast to traditional approaches, in which a small executive group or team develops future directions and strategies and then, through a series of discrete events, tries to bring about acceptance and change.

Before we look at the flow of activities in the actual conference, it is important to examine the underlying principles. The first principle is *to get the whole system, or a representation of that system, into the room at one time.* By "whole system," we mean all the stakeholders of the organization, issue, or community. For an organization, the whole system might include employees, management, customers, suppliers, and regulators. For a school system, it might be teachers, administrators, students, parents, community members, representatives of the district superintendent's office, and taxpayer groups.

The second principle is that *the work that goes on is done in the context of the larger environment,* that is, participants think globally and act locally. In Billie's work on building a Connecticut community "free from fear," it was very useful to see local violence in the context of increasing global violence—for example, how global violence is often pictured on television and how those representations affect perceptions about and levels of violence in the local community.

The third principle is the *emphasis on common ground.* The group will not spend hours haggling about different points. When strong differences arise, if they cannot be worked through in a reasonable amount of time, they will be acknowledged, recorded, and worked through later, outside the conference. The group will move forward only on what everyone can agree on.

The fourth principle is that *groups are self-managing.* With some guidelines, each eight-member group seated around each five-foot-diameter table becomes a self-managing team that directs its own internal processes.

The fifth principle is that *there are no external experts*. The expertise resides within the total group. They provide and analyze the data and work together to create a future.

The sixth principle is that *Future Search is not a problem-solving conference*. Problems may be identified, especially in terms of the present and current reality, but once they have been noted, the group moves to developing an ideal future scenario.

The final principle is that Weisbord and Janoff believe that change involves the whole person: mind, body, and spirit.

Planning for the Conference

Many people consider planning as something to "get through" before they can get to the "real" conference. However, we want to emphasize that in every method covered in this book, planning is a critical factor in the method's success. Thus, the first task in the Future Search Conference is to plan the event. Several planning meetings precede the actual event or, more accurately, the planning meetings actually begin the conference. The planning group has three very important tasks.

First, it must decide on the conference's purpose. Although often a general presenting issue exists, the purpose needs to be defined in such a way that the conference focuses its work on the right issue and the issue is meaningful to the stakeholders who are invited to attend. In planning the Future Search Conference for the urban community in Connecticut, for example, the presenting concern was violence. The planning group sharpened the issue to "building a community free from fear." This broader purpose for the conference kept the group away from problem solving (such as providing more police or counseling centers for domestic violence) and kept the group focused on creating a type of environment that would prevent violence rather than merely trying to control violence where it already existed.

Second, the planning group needs to decide which stakeholders are to be invited. Stakeholders are the people, both inside and outside of the organization, who have a vested interest in the issue being discussed and in its outcome. Choosing stakeholders is a key responsibility, because having the right issue and the right people in the room is critical for success. Planning groups need to be urged to cast a wide net. Later on they can narrow it down to the essential stakeholder groups and the essential people within those groups. Our experience is that as the planning group thinks about which external stakeholders to involve (especially the stakeholders who are not usually included), it begins to see the potential for this type of meeting. External stakeholders bring important insights to the table and are often the major impetus for driving change. Outside stakeholder groups also break up internal collusions and remind the organization of its larger purpose.

Third, the group must plan how the conference results will be carried forward after the conference ends. In communities, this usually involves the creation of an entity that coordinates action and continuing activities. In an organization, it may be either a management responsibility or the work of a continuing, authorized group. However it is structured, having a plan in place is crucial to the long-range success of the conference.

The Conference

After the planning tasks are completed, the Future Search can proceed. Let us look next at the flow of activities or tasks performed within a Future Search Conference and how these tasks contribute to the outcome. The tasks are performed both in small heterogeneous groups as well as in homogeneous groups of stakeholders depending on the topic being addressed. The information generated by these small groups is shared with the whole community. Six major tasks take place during the three-day conference:

1. Focus on our history
2. Focus on the present: current trends

3. Discuss "prouds and sorries"
4. Focus on the future
5. Discover common futures
6. Take action

Day One

Focus on Our History

What has happened at the global level over the last thirty years? What has happened to our organization over the same time span? What has happened to us personally during that time? During this section, long strips of two-by-twenty-four-foot paper are posted on three walls, labeled "Global," "Organization or Issue," and "Personal." These sheets of paper are divided into decades, usually the 1960s through the 1990s or as determined by the planning group. After briefly making notes to themselves, the participants are invited to write their recollections of these time periods on the wall charts. This exercise both is a useful way of validating every person's experience and reminds people that the group's work is part of a longer historical process. It also helps in building a common data base.

In the Connecticut conference, the history actually suggested what needed to be done in the future. It showed the destruction of the community over a fifteen-year period through the building of superhighways, the loss of the state fair, and a series of other events. This suggested that the focus be not on containing violence but on rebuilding community and a sense of the common good.

In another example, when we worked on redesigning an MBA program for a business school, the history reminded everyone in the room how white, middle-class, and insular the business school had been in recent history.

Once the history is posted, heterogenous groups of eight members are asked to interpret one of the wall charts and to look for patterns and insights. This process, which does not use experts, gives the group the experience of working together and establishes confidence in the participants' ability to make sense of a great deal of data.

Focus on the Present

This next task moves from looking at the past to examining the present reality. A giant map is created on the wall with the organization or issue in the middle. The total community calls out the trends that they believe are currently affecting this organization or issue, and the facilitators write these trends on the chart. This giant "mind map" is both stimulating and overwhelming. We usually do not take the time to recognize how many external forces impinge on us! This recognition is often a low moment in the conference as people wonder, "How on earth are we going to make sense of all this?"

It is at this point in the conference that the community begins, as Weisbord says, to engage the chaos. What happens here is that as participants recognize that their pet solutions (everyone has them) will not work, they also recognize that they are "all stuck in this together." The realization comes that they cannot cope alone. Saul Alinsky (1946), the famous community organizer, was fond of saying that your enemy (the external forces) organizes for you. That is, outside forces create pressure for change and push people to organize. It is owning the complexity and struggling with it that seems to encourage community.

The second part of looking at the current reality is to ask the group to highlight what they see as the most important factors affecting the issue or organization. People use colored sticky dots to "vote" for the most important forces. The group will probably end up with seven to ten priorities. If the Future Search has started in the early afternoon, as Weisbord and Janoff recommend, this is the end of the first day and participants go home for "soak time" to absorb what has happened thus far. (Weisbord uses the expression *soak time* to emphasize the importance of taking a break in the work and allowing time to absorb and reflect.)

Day Two

The second day begins as the stakeholder groups select one of the priorities to work on in more detail. In these groups, discussion focuses on "What are we currently doing about this trend and what would we like to do?" In the Connecticut community's conference on building a community free from fear, most groups picked the breakdown of the family system as an important factor affecting the community. As the groups explored the causes of this breakdown, what they were currently doing, and what they would like to do, it became apparent that the breakdown had to be seen in the larger context of the breakdown of the community, or, as one of the participants reported, quoting African folk wisdom, "It takes an entire village to raise a child."

Discuss "Prouds and Sorries"

At this point in the conference, participants ask themselves, "What do we feel proud about and sorry about in relation to our conference theme?" and "What are the implications of this information for the present and the future?"

This, the last step in looking at current reality, is, in our opinion, a very important point in the conference. People are still working in stakeholder groups, but a curious shift takes place, which we call the shift from "me" to "we"—from *my* department, or *my* agency, to the good of the whole. During this exercise, groups start owning up to and assuming responsibility for what they have done and not done. They now have a better understanding of the whole system, internal as well as external. It becomes clear that, to improve the whole, the different parts of the system will have to take responsibility for maximizing the whole, as opposed to maximizing their part to the detriment of the other parts.

The insights that can grow out of stakeholder feedback and taking responsibility were demonstrated in the Future Search Conference we conducted for the university's MBA program. For some time, a major source of conflict had been whether more emphasis should be on the so-called "soft" sciences, such as management and organizational behavior, or the traditional "hard" sciences, such as statistics and finance. This conflict had created tremendous tensions in the business school, which in turn began to have an impact on the quality of its offerings to students and the business community. Feedback from businesspeople outside the school emphasized that its polarization of the issue was completely off base. What the outside stakeholders perceived was that organizational behavior components *plus* the financial and more quantitative areas combined to create a winning program. In addition, they wanted to see more than just hard and soft sciences; they wanted interdisciplinary cases, team teaching, programs that would reflect not just local but global economics, and much stronger partnerships with the business community.

Given this information, participants were able to see the current reality and acknowledge how their action or inaction had contributed to the program's conflict and its inability to respond to the needs of its community. For these participants, this section was a moment when everyone—the alumni, students, and faculty—shared, in a nonblaming fashion, their enormous disappointments about and dreams for the program.

During the conference in the Connecticut community, an important moment was reached when the social service agencies acknowledged in their "sorries" that they were ashamed of how much time they had spent fighting each other over decreased funding rather than working together to eliminate duplications in programs and discover ways to better serve the community's needs.

Focus on the Future

In this phase, scenarios (skits) of our ideal future are developed and presented. Returning to the heterogeneous groups, participants brainstorm their ideal future and then develop and present scenarios of that future. This is an enormously energizing activity because peo-

ple literally have to place themselves in that future. In the Connecticut community, many of the skits dramatized such things as schools
and community centers that held classes for adults as well as providing community meeting space, mobile health units that delivered
services in neighborhoods, churches that opened their doors during
the week for day care, tutoring programs, and classes in English as
a second language, with many programs being staffed with retired
people and volunteers. One scenario envisioned every neighborhood
having safe, accessible outdoor space for recreational activities.

Discover Common Futures

The next phase is to identify the common themes across all the
scenarios and integrate them into one list. When this has been
accomplished, the total community reviews its common themes.
Any item for which conflict or disagreement emerges is placed on a
"disagree" list. The facilitator continually makes it clear to the participants that they should move ahead only on what they can agree
on and are willing to support. Support is more than just saying,
"That's a good idea. Somebody should do it." Support means that
each person or stakeholder group would be willing to work on that
particular theme. This is another important moment. Our experience is that if the consultant or the group pushes for closure too
quickly, people may agree to what, in fact, they are not ready or
willing to support. What has surprised us, however, is not the number of "disagree" items but rather how much commonality exists
in these future scenarios. This work ends the second day in the
traditional three-day time frame.

Day Three

Take Action

This phase, which begins the morning of the third day, is when
action plans emerge out of the common themes. This is yet another

crucial moment in the conference because out of the commitment to these common futures springs commitment to action.

It is important to note that if Future Search is run in two days instead of three, the group comes to this point at the end of the second day. Not surprisingly, the group is exhausted, right at a time when it must summon energy to work in a much more linear mode. For this reason, we agree with Weisbord and Janoff in exhorting people to use a three-day conference that starts around midday on the first day and ends at midday on the third day. Although it also takes two days, the extra night allows reflection time, or soak time, for people to assimilate large amounts of information and to be ready at the end of the conference to move toward implementing actions.

Several approaches are available for planning for the future, or action planning. In one format, participants in stakeholder groups agree on future actions that their stakeholder groups will take, given the strategic goals that have been selected. These action commitments are shared with the entire community. The MBA program used another format, in which people self-selected future initiatives they wished to work on and formed task groups to deal with the chosen initiative. They planned both short- and long-term action steps. Then, they decided who might need to be included in future meetings and when the next meeting would be. These plans were shared with the total community.

In action planning groups within the Connecticut community, the participants, after reaching agreement on the future goals, posted these goals on separate sheets of newsprint around the room. Each person in the room brainstormed her or his ideas as to how these goals might be achieved and placed the ideas (written on Post-it Notes™) under the appropriate goal. People then self-selected the future initiative they wanted to work on. Groups were formed, with each group receiving, as "seeds," the notes posted for their goal. This gave a high level of ownership for all the initiatives and used the creative resources of the entire community.

Questions About Future Search

The previous section illustrated the flow of the standard and tested design, as well as providing examples of each step in the process. Now we will answer some of the questions that people most frequently ask us about Future Search.

What about follow-up?
In their early work, Weisbord and Janoff believed that the energy generated by the conference process created the necessary follow-up actions. They also believed strongly that the implementation of action plans is not a consultant-driven task but rather is the participants' responsibility. This is in sharp contrast to most consultant-led interventions.

Many people have expressed concern about follow-up after these events. When we discussed the impact of action plan follow-up with someone who had run over fifteen conferences, he made an interesting comment: "Follow-up actions may have to do more with the culture of the back-home organization than with the time spent in action planning." If, after a highly successful conference, people move back into strongly bureaucratic organizations, they run the risk of either being co-opted by the system or running into functional and bureaucratic stone walls.

Weisbord and Janoff now suggest follow-up actions such as alumni reunions that include newcomers, six-month or periodic review sessions, and newsletters, to coordinate actions and inform people about what is going on and to give them a venue for providing feedback to each other. We agree that this issue is critical, not only for this method but for some of the other methods covered in this book. Sometimes, follow-up activities spontaneously continue, changes are made, and task groups are formed to bring the changes into being. But at other times, after an inspiring conference, the momentum just fizzles.

As we look back on the Future Search Conferences we have

been involved in, some ideas about follow-up stand out. In the university MBA redesign, a follow-up structure already existed around curriculum redesign, so the information generated in the Future Search went to the curriculum committee. The dean also took responsibility for making sure that task forces would be supported and information on progress would be shared with the larger community. As a result, several months after the conference, the following was reported in the local newspaper: team teaching, with cases that cut across disciplines; strong alliances with the business community (with businesspeople coming into the university and teaching a class); internships in businesses for both students and faculty; a curriculum that represented global awareness; and courses that dealt with cross-cultural understanding.

In the community in Connecticut, a follow-up meeting was held three months later to find out what the various task forces were doing and to see if additional resources were needed. Some of the task forces had added new members, and some of the more modest short-term goals had already become reality. More meetings were planned to work on the broader issues.

Are some organizations better able to use this type of approach than others? Weisbord and Janoff have been particularly committed to working in the public sector, although this method is not confined to that area. Fortune 500 companies as well as school systems and communities are using this approach. Many Future Search Conferences do occur in the not-for-profit sector. Since the process is nonhierarchical and egalitarian, we think that the diffusion of power in the public sector lends itself more readily to this approach. In communities, it is clear that with funding diminishing, agencies need to collaborate and work together. Future Search is well suited to help with this issue. However, in some situations, Future Search would probably not be the intervention of choice, for example:

- In organizations where the leadership has a high need for control

- Where the workforce is so alienated from management that workers would not be willing to participate

- If the organization already has a clear and compelling future vision

- In a situation where a subsidiary, department, or division has little opportunity for choice about the future because the decisions are controlled by the larger organization, such as corporate headquarters

Can Future Search be effectively done with more than 70 people?
Weisbord and Janoff believe that 70 to 80 people are the ideal number, and we agree. With more than 70 people, Future Search tends to lose the face-to-face quality and the sense of community of the event. With fewer than 40, it lacks the multiple perspectives from the stakeholders. The limits, however, are being stretched. We have talked to a number of consultants who are convinced that the benefit of having more stakeholders present outweighs a potential loss of community. We also know of a few conferences that have successfully included over 150 people.

We would also add that the face-to-face quality of a Future Search Conference is really achieved at the tables of eight, because these max-mix tables (heterogenous groups crossing levels and functions) are a microcosm of the community. However, if the total participants number more than seventy, table reports of discussions to the total community would become tedious and time-consuming, requiring a different method.

The other process that Weisbord and Janoff recommend and that has been successful is the multisearch conference, made up of a number of concurrently running Future Searches, which allows more people to be included. In a recent health care system Future Search Conference, five different hospitals that were part of the same system held five Future Search Conferences in five separate rooms in the same facility. Of course, the data from these simultaneous conferences had to be integrated, but, as the consultants reported to us, the similarity of the output was amazing and little work was required to integrate the themes.

Does this approach translate well into cultures outside the United States?
We know that this approach is currently being used in the Americas, Asia, Europe, and Australia. We have talked with consultants all over the world, and they say that the process seems to be well suited to their countries. At times, of course, the language needs to be modified for cultural reasons. For example, a consultant who ran a Future Search Conference with the Inuit in northwestern Canada changed "prouds and sorries" to "successes and missed opportunities." We also understand that these terms had to be phrased differently in Germany. When we ran a conference in Venezuela, people reported that they would have preferred to talk the history rather than write it, which may have resulted from the strength and importance of the oral tradition in that community. Consultants using Future Search in other countries have often integrated certain culturally appropriate customs into the conference, for example, drumming, dancing, traditional games, mariachi bands, singing, and daily reflection and meditation.

Why not start with the analysis of the present? Is the history piece important?
Recently we were talking to a person who wanted to run Future Search Conferences in Israel, in organizations where Arabs and Jews work together. As we described the history part of the design, we were aware that this could be a critical issue and we were not surprised when the person expressed reservations. "We could never do this," he said. "We would get stuck in history forever. We are *already* stuck in history." When we discussed this matter with Weisbord and Janoff, they felt that the history dilemma should be raised, discussed, and worked out with the planning committee, who might decide that the history issue would be too volatile for this group.

On the other hand, after running a conference in Mexico, Ernesto Poza reported, "It was moving and powerful to see the turbulent history of Mexico on the walls of the room. The discovery of the community was that at the national as well as the individual level, they had survived horrendous times!" This historical record developed by the group was a testimony to their courage and survival skills. Rather than being seen as negative, it brought hope and confidence in their ability to manage fundamental change.

Questions About the Search Conference and Future Search

Many people we have talked to who have implemented either Search Conferences or Future Search, whether they occurred with school systems in California, community groups working on environmental issues, the Inuit in the Northwest Territories, or business organizations, have expressed appreciation for these processes. We feel that both methods have a powerful flow that creates energy for concerted action toward a better future. Following are some reflections on the two types of conference, based on questions we frequently hear.

What is the difference between the Search Conference and Future Search?
Weisbord and Janoff (Future Search) base much of their work on Emery and Trist's method (Search Conference). They were also influenced by the work of Ronald Lippitt. The roots of the two types of conference are similar, as are some of the underlying philosophies and theories. The same topics (turbulent environment, history, desired future) are covered, but they use different methods and groupings and a different order. In the Search Conference, most of the work is done in the large group. Future Search has more of a mixture of large and small groups. Both work toward desired futures. In terms of the methods used, we would say that Future Search uses more evocative methods, and the Search Conference uses more rational methods (which may also generate a significant amount of creative thinking and activity).

We feel that there is little difference in how these methods handle community settings, and outcomes from community groups seem similar in both approaches. The differences we notice are in the approach they use with organizations. The Search Conference has a stronger focus on democratizing the workplace and on the way work gets managed. The Future Search focus is on generating collaborative action toward a desired future, not necessarily toward a more democratic way of doing work in the organization, although the method's originators would certainly not be opposed to that. In talking to people who have used the Search Conference method in manufacturing plants or in divisions of companies, we find that they often follow the conference with Participative Design (see Chapter Ten), which focuses on the work system itself using a definite set of theories and criteria for redesign work.

Is the approach to conflict the same in both methods?
We believe that, for the most part, it is. Both approaches emphasize common ground. Although conflict is not avoided, the way these conferences are designed does not necessarily move people toward conflict. They have an understanding, from the start, that the group will move ahead only on those items that everyone can agree on. In Future Search, disagreements are acknowledged and posted, and then the group moves on. Merrelyn Emery uses the term "rationalization of conflict." In the Search Conference, when conflicts appear, they are discussed and clarified. When an issue cannot be worked out in a reasonable period of time, it is acknowledged and recorded on a "disagree" list to be dealt with after the conference. The group then moves on to what they can agree on. It is our impression, however, that the Emery Search Conference spends more time confronting and trying to work through conflict than Future Search. What people often discover after experiencing these two methods is how much they *do* agree.

Is the approach to follow-up the same with both methods?
The Search Conference devotes a third of the conference to follow-up action planning, which generally means a whole day. With the

Future Search Conference, usually three to four hours on the final day are devoted to action planning.

Are these really large-scale, whole-system interventions, when only thirty-five to forty people are involved?
The Search Conference usually focuses on a work system agenda, whereas the Future Search Conference often focuses on the entire organization or a large portion of it. For a Search Conference, if thirty-five to forty people make up a significant portion of the work system being addressed, then that number is considered "whole system" and sufficient. On the other hand, if a Future Search is dealing with a systemic, organization-wide change, the number of participants needed to represent that aspect of the system may, of necessity, be larger, because each person represents an aspect of the system, bringing a perspective that is needed to see the whole. It is important not to get fixated on absolute numbers but instead to remember the key concept of representation. Getting a critical mass, or multiple perspectives, in the room may require forty people for one organization and its task but need seventy-five or more people for another organization and its task.

It is also important to remember that both the Search Conference and the Future Search Conference can use "multisearch," in which simultaneous or sequential groups meet around the same issue and thus allow an organization to include and handle more people, logistically, than they thought they could. For example, in the Crestone, Colorado, conference, multisearch allowed three conferences, with a total of 150 people, to occur simultaneously. With any multisearch, the key is to collate and disseminate the data so that everyone is fully informed.

Why are external stakeholders not included (Search Conference) when work is being done within an organization?
Merrelyn Emery considers outside stakeholders to be a part of the environment whose opinions should be sought and reported, but feels that only people who will have *direct responsibility* for implementation should have seats at the conference. Other consultants

and organizations we have talked to draw a much wider boundary of the system. As an example, for a large chemical company that used the Emery Search Conference, the issue was customer and supplier relations; stakeholders were therefore seen as an integral part of the system and included in the conference.

In addition, we have noted that today's customers and suppliers not only have opinions and feedback; they are often highly involved with some of the implementation plans. At the Boeing Company, for example, customers were involved in significant design modifications of the 777 aircraft. Our experience is that customer views are very crucial to getting the system to change. Very often, when customers are included in these events, customer-company task forces are established, supplier councils are formed, and critical new information that benefits everyone is shared across company, customer, and supplier boundaries. In a recent Future Search Conference in a school district, the presence of a taxpayer's organization at the conference was very helpful in making sure that an educational bond issue passed. In another instance, in a Search Conference, a sales group included a marketing representative who was helpful not only in sharing important data but also in helping to implement change in the marketing function.

It is worth considering the Emerys' point here: the people in the room should be those who are going to be *responsible* for implementation. Certainly, various ways exist to bring in the outside data other than having outside stakeholders physically present—*if* all we are after is information. We have seen, however, that outside stakeholders can suddenly become important allies, which reminds us to think carefully about how to draw the boundaries.

Chapter Five

Real Time Strategic Change

The largest group that we observed involved eight hundred employees of a utility company with ten thousand employees. It was the third large group event the company had sponsored as part of a system-wide change effort that is still continuing. Here is our description of the event.

Day One

There is an air of anticipation as people arrive at the huge, rectangular auditorium, some even well before the 8:00 A.M. start. Upbeat music is coming in over the sound system. Continental breakfasts are laid out in a number of locations so that they are easy to pick up. Maps of the auditorium with table numbers make it easy to find your preassigned table and meet your max-mix table group of eight. Each round table is five feet in diameter, just the right distance across for easy conversation.

Robert Jacobs, from Dannemiller / Tyson consulting firm of Ann Arbor, has been working with the twenty-four-person design team for this event for several months. It includes two external and two internal consultants. The design team is representative of all levels and functions in the organization. The purpose of this three-day meeting is to endorse or modify a mission and values statement that will position the organization to deal with the increasingly competitive environment, to identify current practices and behaviors that are consistent and inconsistent with this mission and values, and to plan how to take action to bring the way the organization operates in line with the mission and values—in other words, to change the culture from bureaucratic to more responsive, participative, and competitive.

The design team has worked closely with the consultants to plan a design that will accomplish this task, often trying out pieces of it themselves. They also created a logistics team of thirty people, who spent yesterday setting up the auditorium and who now, in a precisely orchestrated ballet of managed details, will ensure the seamless delivery of materials to tables, microphones to speakers, and lunches to everyone.

A hush gradually quells the noise of eight hundred people animatedly talking to each other. We notice that the podium is now occupied. Huge video screens in different parts of the room carry this image so everyone can see that we are about to begin.

We are welcomed by two members of the design team who also represent the union-management partnership in planning this event. They are informal but direct. They tell us why we are here, what has preceded this event, and what work needs to be done here. Then the president of the company and the head of the union welcome us and talk about the importance of this meeting to them. Finally, the two consultants who will run the meeting with members of the design team are introduced and we are ready for a short introductory activity at the tables.

This sets the pattern. No long speeches are given. Short inputs are followed by discussion of specific questions at the tables. The roles of facilitator, recorder, reporter, and timekeeper rotate with each table task. In this case, each table records what people say they need in order to make the meeting worthwhile. These statements are posted around the walls as people take a short coffee break, so that it is easy to read what other tables have said.

The rest of the morning is spent sharing information and stimulating thinking about the business environment the organization faces. A panel that includes experts on the industry, government regulators, and customers paints the picture outside the organization. After discussion, a panel of insiders gives its views on the internal challenges that face the company. An important moment is the presentation by a customer who did not select this company as a vendor. Questions from the floor come at him with intensity as people begin to figure out what went wrong.

The morning is intended as mutual education: the participants all must understand the business environment that affects them. After lunch, they discuss "What's working and what's not working in our company?" Tables brainstorm lists of "glads, sads, and mads" from their work experience. Again, these are posted around the room and everyone gets a crayon to check his or her top five priorities on the wall charts. Then a volunteer team of "synthesizers" reviews the charts, pulls out the most popular items, and reports them back to the entire group. It is really quite amazing to see eight hundred people working together like this—and enjoying it!

The rest of the afternoon is a process of reviewing and confirming or questioning the mission, vision, values, and key strategies that were developed at a previous five-hundred-person three-day event. This is done through short inputs and table discussions. People stand and clap when they agree and report any major "hiccups" that represent problems. Generally, because these ideas come to them already shaped by the workforce, they are supported well, with only a few emendations. The evaluation of the day is brainstormed onto flip charts as "the pluses and minuses of today" and posted as input to the design team, which continues to meet throughout the event to confirm or adjust the design.

Day Two

The first part of the morning is given over to finally confirming the mission and values and the key work on strategies of the previous day. Then, once firm agreement has been reached and all the "hiccups" have been responded to, the group spends the rest of the morning creating a picture of success and what would need to happen internally to make it achievable. They do this in an interactive process at tables, using Post-it Notes, brainstorming, and prioritizing in a stepped series of activities whose final product is a chart for each table of the most important processes, procedures, and policies that need to change to ensure the new vision. Everyone then gets five sticky dots to use in voting on the wall charts for what she or he considers to be the most important issues. While the participants have lunch, the synthesizers count the dots and identify the top issues.

After lunch, everyone is invited to select one of these issues to work on in a new group. Large signs identify where each issue group will meet and people create new tables of eight to do this work. After they are given a process for analyzing the current situation, they make recommendations for change. When these recommendations are posted around the walls, each person is given twenty gummed stars to show his or her own priorities for change. These are announced, the day is evaluated, and most of the participants depart.

This is a critical point in the design, because now a joint team of company officers and union officers goes to work on the recommendations. They work through the evening and into the small hours of the morning, deciding what they can do, where the leverage points are, what cannot be implemented and why, and how to be ready to report back first thing on the third day. At the same time, the design team is meeting to make adjustments in the next day's design.

Day Three

The day begins with a report from the design team about the activities of last evening. Then the joint officers come forward to make their report. They begin by describing what they will support and work on, what must be decided contractually, and what will not fly. In the process, they announce two policy changes concerning egregious policies that were disliked by many. They are wiping the slate clean and their decision is greeted by waves of applause and a hall on its feet yelling and cheering. A feeling of movement and change is in the air!

The next hour is spent at max-mix tables in an activity that identifies helpful norms that need to be strengthened ("Keep the customer focus") and dysfunctional organizational norms that need to change if the vision and values are to be realized ("Stop finger pointing and blaming others"). Then, groups are asked to suggest a new positive norm that should replace the dysfunctional one. As these are reported, people clap if they agree.

The bulk of the day is spent in people's real business-unit groups in a process that selects the highest-priority issues for their unit, plans action steps, and makes real commitments to change. They also make commitments about cross-functional issues in implementing change. By mid-afternoon, a great deal of work has been done and people are clearly getting very tired. After reports of this work and of commitments that have been made, the final event is to think about all the other members of the company who were not here and how to include them. Teams are proposed to take the message back. People are asked to volunteer to help by signing up, and 450 people sign up! The day ends on a note of personal commitments at table groups, statements of union and management commitments from the platform, and an evaluation asking about participants' confidence in the change and ways to keep the momentum going.

Since this event, which was judged very successful just after it ended, the work on internalizing the mission and values in every employee has gone on in several ways. In the context of the overall strategic framework and encouraged by the leadership team, departments have measured themselves and identified levers for change. The new performance development process, which includes feedback from subordinates, peers, and boss, incorporates the values in its measurement system and training support is provided. An employee survey is being used to track progress. These activities are clearly related to the work on mission and values and to key management strategies, but whether individuals see them as part of the same process is uncertain. The paradigm shift that occurred during this event must also happen in the larger organization if this change effort is to be successful. For many people, being there in the room with eight hundred others is the emotional touchstone. Those who were not there do not share the same experience.

Real Time Strategic Change

The vignette just described illustrates the core type of change process that was originally created by Kathleen Dannemiller with Chuck Tyson, Al Davenport, and Bruce Gibb in work at Ford Motor Company and, more recently, with her colleague, Robert Jacobs (Jacobs, 1994). The underlying philosophy as well as some of the creative design units were inspired by Ronald Lippitt, who was for many years a professor at the University of Michigan. Lippitt trained many of the senior organization development professionals currently in practice. He had a very close mentoring relationship with Kathleen Dannemiller over many years and was a great influence in her life and on her professional values and practice.

Unlike the methods we have presented thus far, Real Time Strategic Change (RTSC) is not a process that has one clear outcome. Both the Search Conference and Future Search help organizations agree on a common direction. The four work design methods shown on page 31 create a new organizational structure. In contrast to this, RTSC is a participative process for involving the whole system in planning for change. The change objectives in RTSC, however, can be anything from a new strategic direction or a new organizational design to planning for mergers or for a different culture at work. In this chapter, we are using RTSC to describe interventions dealing with future planning. In Chapter Nine, we describe this method combined with Socio-Technical Systems to design or redesign organizations.

The same method can also be used to solve problems, sense issues, coordinate intergroup activities, and fulfill a host of other purposes. When it is used for these latter purposes, RTSC goes by the term Large Scale Interactive Events and is appropriate to Part Four of this book. Because the methods are essentially the same, even though the objectives may differ, we will discuss them only in this chapter. RTSC is a multipurpose method that can be used to involve people participatively at any point in the continuum of planning and enacting. Of course, there are limits to the outcomes worth convening the whole organization to consider. Usually, issues need to be critical in the life and functioning of the whole system, ones that are important to everyone's future at work.

If RTSC can be used for a number of objectives, what are the critical markers that distinguish this method from others? We think that four critical underlying dimensions are central to understanding and being able to think about RTSC.

Size

Although it is certainly true that all the methods we are describing in this book are very participative, the creators of RTSC had a fundamental commitment to democracy that pervades their work. More specifically, they had the optimistic view of human nature that people are energized by knowing more and having the opportunity to participate in setting their own destiny. This view is also shared, in varying degrees of intensity, by other methods.

What is unique about participation as practiced by the Dannemiller group and Robert Jacobs, founder of Five Oceans International, is size. They have created the technology to allow thousands of people to participate in decision making in one place and at one time. Unlike some other methods, theirs is not limited to 80 or so people at a time. They can and do take a whole 2,200-person factory off-site for three days to set their strategic vision. At this point, they may have reached the upper limit (although in our experience, it is more usual for companies to hold meetings of between 300 and 900 people). They have also held simultaneous meetings of 1,500 employees at each of three dispersed sites that were linked by telecommunications.

As a result of their work with very large numbers of people, they have developed to a fine art the logistics that must accompany a seamless meeting. They have strategies for working with hotels, have created the role of logistics "czar," train the logistics team in advance of each event, and include in their workbook the logistics instructions that are essential to each design. (See the Appendix for information on this workbook.)

Degrees of Authority

Another defining characteristic is the capacity of RTSC to allow those in authority, the top management of the organization in question, to decide how much of their power and control they want to trust to others. This method is flexible with regard to how much decision-making power management relinquishes. In the utility company example that began this chapter, management was able to set the constraints within which participation occurred. At their earlier five-hundred-person event, top management came to the large event with a straw statement of their vision, values, and strategy. After some education and a lot of discussion, they took what they heard from their people and revised their document, integrating the feedback they received from the organization. If they did not accept an idea, they had to say why. This process was so satisfactory that they decided to do another iteration with nearly 10 percent of the company in order to be sure that a critical mass understood and endorsed the new direction and strategy.

Typically, the outcome is highly satisfactory to those who give the input. They feel that their voice has been heard and their views have been taken very seriously and incorporated. This then releases the energy to plan and implement actions that will make the new strategy a reality. Thus, in RTSC, management accepts influence from others about the future strategic direction of the company.

In another use of RTSC, at Marriott Corporation (Dannemiller and Jacobs, 1992), the strategy of continuous improvement had already been decided upon, but quality tools were taught at an RTSC event in order to enable each hotel to use them to identify, understand, and solve critical problems that were affecting the quality of service delivery. In other words, people had a voice in what needed to improve and how to do it, but not in the overall direction of change.

During the contracting phase, the consultants discussed with management what would be expected of them, particularly in letting go of power and becoming more vulnerable by really listening to their employees. Managements that want to continue making decisions in the old command-and-control paradigm will find that this technology will not work. In fact, it is likely to cause public damage to the management's credibility. It is therefore recommended that management carefully search their own hearts to be sure that they are ready to share decision-making power before signing up.

Creating a Shared Framework

In actuality, we think that all of these methods help the entire system to talk to itself and get everyone "reading off the same sheet," or, as the Dannemiller group puts it, "create a common data base" (Jacobs, 1994, p. 56). This sounds very much like what Senge (1990) is talking about in *The Fifth Discipline*. If the whole system is to become able to change and adapt to a turbulent environment, a necessary first step is for the people in it to understand the environment and its likely impact on their organization. Before you can think strategically, you need a common understanding of the situation you are in. In open systems planning (Jayaram, 1977), organizations do both an environmental analysis and an internal analysis to get a fix on their situation. In the first day of most RTSC events, planned inputs and activities enable everyone to hear from the outside world, including customers, and from each other. The max-mix group structure at round tables of eight is designed to bring people into contact with others outside of their normal contacts in the system. They are encouraged to recognize and value the different perspectives that are expressed. This creates a microcosm of the organization at each table. As each table becomes an effective work group, the capacity of the organization to act together increases.

Thus, this model emphasizes that everyone should understand the views of management, the employees, and the outside world. Wide sharing of information creates a common data base, which then enables the group to act with "one heart and one mind."

The System-Wide Paradigm Shift

Dannemiller consultants talk about what a large group feels like after a "paradigm shift" has occurred. This is a process that is easiest to describe at the individual level. What usually happens to people who attend these events is that they arrive interested but skeptical, maybe even hostile, a bit uncertain about why they are there and what will happen. In the early phases, they learn a lot but they are often not convinced that the event is anything more than a big boondoggle. Often, they are skeptical about management's intentions and whether what is being said is more than just the usual management talk. In the process of the first two days of work together, as they watch management respond and as they find their own voice, they feel more hopeful, energized, and excited about the possibility of a changed and better future. This gives them energy to help things change for the better. When management begins to act in significant ways to improve the work situation, make real decisions that affect individuals positively, and do this as a result of employee input, the response by members of the system is a flow of energy focused on taking their own actions to make the shared and desired future real. When this happens to many people in the same place, the energy in the room changes noticeably and a paradigm shift occurs. This is really what empowerment is about. People feel that they are not pawns but actors affecting their own destiny.

The Theory Base of Real Time Strategic Change

RTSC creates a custom-tailored design or flow of events for each new situation. Of course, many activities, discussion processes, and materials have been perfected over time and are used repeatedly. The state of the system as analyzed using change theory determines the flow of events.

The Dannemiller group have made Gleicher's change formula (Beckhard and Harris, 1987) a centerpiece of the way they think about the design flow of a large group event. The formula:

$$C = D \times V \times F > R$$

states that change (C) will occur when sufficient dissatisfaction (D) with the current organizational system exists, when everyone has a clear vision (V) of the organizational goals for the future, and when it is clear what first steps (F) can be taken to move the system in the direction of the vision. All three elements must be in place and must be greater than the resistance to change (R) that is present in the organization in order for change to occur. If any element is not present—if, for example, the organization has no clear vision—people may be stuck in their dissatisfaction and not know how to act. Or, if the organization has a vision but no first steps, people may want to change but feel frustrated about what to do.

Dissatisfaction

Dissatisfaction is critical because it destabilizes or "unfreezes" the situation (Lewin, 1943). When people lose the comfort of the status quo and become uncomfortable, they are interested in finding ways to improve their situation and are more open to change. Although we all know a few people who take pleasure in wallowing in their gripes and complaints, most people want to be working productively at something that they feel is worthwhile.

The Dannemiller group has worked with an interesting range of clients in terms of their level of dissatisfaction; this, of course, affects the design. In systems where change is needed but many employees are quite content with business as usual, the dissatisfaction has to be created within the RTSC event. At Corning Inc., for example, in the early days of a joint effort between management and shop-floor workers to make manufacturing sites more productive, workers often did not realize how much the world had changed or the jeopardy their plant was in. When they heard important customers leveling with them about their own business pressures and their unhappiness over poor quality or price, it got their attention. They began to realize that business as usual might not be an option. In King County, Washington, at METRO, the transportation provider for the Seattle, little awareness existed of the treatment that women and minorities often endured at work. A major culture change was needed. One method that was used to create more awareness of what was occurring in the organization was to ask women and minorities to "tell their stories" early in the event. This created a shared data base about what the situation really was and raised both awareness and dissatisfaction (Jacobs, 1994, pp. 184–186).

In some organizations, dissatisfaction is already present and is carried into the event with virtually every participant. This was the case at a conference held at the Corning Revere Ware plant, which is described in Chapter Nine. The plant had been acquired by Corning relatively recently and had a very troubled labor history during the 1980s, when it was sold several times. Workers arrived full of skepticism and unhappiness and full of ideas about changes that were needed. A quite different situation existed in New York City, where, in an effort to address the increasing rate of tuberculosis, especially among homeless and indigent populations, the Fund for the City of New York used RTSC to bring together representatives of all the agencies, the public hospital system, and centers that participated in service delivery to those at risk or with TB (Jacobs,

1994, pp. 258–261). The rate of increase of TB was making the national news; therefore, it seemed reasonable to suppose that most of the people who came to the conference were dissatisfied with the current state of effectiveness of the system and ready to find ideas for improving it.

Dissatisfaction is a continuum. In RTSC, a steering committee of representative system members and consultants assesses where the system is and what needs to happen for people to be ready to change. Typical design elements that are used to expose dissatisfaction or create a sense of shared dissatisfaction include customer input, inclusion of industry experts, and simulations. The whole group engages in an organizational diagnosis in which they record what they are proud of in their work and also what they feel sorry about; they then vote on their "proudest prouds" and "sorriest sorries." The "sorries" represent shared dissatisfaction.

Vision

Vision is the clear sense of overall direction that every member of the organization needs and that guides behavior. In many organizations, direction setting is an important function of the leadership. At the same time, everyone in the organization needs to be committed. One way to increase both understanding and commitment is employee participation. This can mean reacting to and having input into top management's vision or it can mean jointly creating the vision with top management. In the Seattle METRO event, the whole system generated the behaviors they wanted to encourage and those that were not acceptable in the organization. Everyone participated in coming to this agreement. At the State College, Pennsylvania, Corning Asahi Video plant, top management brought in their draft of the strategic vision for the plant. After all groups had an opportunity to give their input, management worked most of the night to return to the conference with a revised vision that took account of the feedback they had received.

The employee response was a standing ovation (Jacobs, 1994, pp. 174–177). At the New York City TB event, vision was not a central issue in the design because everyone generally agreed that the goal was to reduce the spread of TB in every way possible. The real issues were how to do it.

First Steps

The New York City TB example focuses on implementation issues. What are the best ways to coordinate to reduce TB? What action should we take? How and when should we take action? In any intervention, it is critical to have some planning for action and clarity about responsibilities. Most events end with both action planning and commitments to change. These commitments can be individual, functional, or cross-functional.

One innovative "first steps" activity that the Dannemiller group uses is called "valentines." Each organizational department or function gets together and decides what it needs from each of the other departments in order to be able to do its own work in a way that achieves the organization's vision. The departments can ask others to start doing new things, stop doing some things, or continue doing certain things. When all departments are ready, the messages are written out, signed by the originating department, and delivered. After the other departments have had time to read and digest the valentines, they make a public statement about what valentines they received and what they plan to do about them. In one company, this process was so useful that for several years, on the fourteenth of every month, valentines were written and delivered as a way of improving progress toward the company's goals.

Greater Than the Resistance to Change

When the first three elements are in place, the paradigm shift we previously described can and does occur. This converts the energy from resistance to change to positive energy for change.

The Role of the Steering Committee in Planning an Event

A steering committee that is representative of all the levels and stakeholders of the organization convenes with the consultants to make all the important decisions about who should attend, to discuss and influence the consultants' design proposals, and to provide information about the organization. The committee helps to estimate the readiness of the system for the proposed event; this, in turn, helps the consultants to propose a design flow that will allow people to participate in the event and achieve the desired goals.

The consultants try out the design on the steering committee and revise it in terms of their reactions. Consensus is the decision-making process that guides the work of the steering committee. Because the consultants sit as members of the steering committee, they also are part of whatever consensus is achieved. This creates an interesting balance of expertise. The organization's representatives are expert about the organization; the consultants are expert about change management and design processes. Together they work out the best fit between these knowledge areas.

Does Real Time Strategic Change Work?

When thousands come together at the cost of much time, labor, and expense, the natural next question is often about results. Was it worth the cost? Did it pay off? Robert Jacobs's book, *Real Time Strategic Change* (1994), is full of anecdotal evidence that exciting and money-saving decisions emerge from these events. Yet the outcomes that are desired differ depending on the client. Some want bottom-line product improvement, whereas others are more interested in alignment around the company's strategic vision. Almost no hard research has been done on tracking effects or comparing the costs and benefits of any large group intervention. Moreover, research on these types of very complex and large-scale events would be difficult and costly to do. One useful strategy for prospective clients is to talk with other companies that have experience with these methods.

We would like to suggest two results-oriented questions that are additional indicators of success:

1. Did the organization use these methods more than once? We believe that when systems come back for more, they at least believe that something useful is happening. This should not be the only test, because systems can also act mindlessly. But there is evidence, at Boeing and Ford, for example— large organizations with years of history using RTSC—that after several large group successes, the system recognized these methods as serving their purposes well and used them repeatedly.

2. Is the system training its own internal people in these methods? When an organization recognizes the usefulness of these methods, it often wants its internal organization development specialists to have these competencies. Practitioners of the methods described in this book all provide training seminars on these methods. Many people employed by companies are now developing these competencies and doing innovative work.

Real Time Strategic Change is a flexible method that can be used to design very large-scale events that create the future, redesign work (see Chapter Nine), or deal with current decisions, problems, and issues in the work system. It is the only method that is included in all three "method" parts of this book.

Chapter Six

ICA Strategic Planning Process

One summer day, a representative from the Quebec Provincial government arrived at the village of Nemaska in northern Quebec and read a letter to the community.

The letter informed the Nemaska band (a branch of the Cree tribe) of the plan to build a huge hydroelectric dam that would raise the water level twenty-three feet and thus flood their village. The suggestion was made that the band resettle in two other Cree villages, which implied breaking up the band. The people were shocked, confused, pained, and angry.

The representative left, and the band had no further news about when or how the dam project would happen, although they heard plenty of rumors. Two years later, the situation was made even more uncertain by the closing of the Hudson Bay store in the Nemaska village, which left the residents without any source of supplies and increased their motivation to relocate to the two Cree villages to the south. As a result, the village was abandoned; the village chief, George Wapachee, moved south to one of the two Cree villages; and two of the council members moved to the other village.

The Cree leadership stated that only beavers had the right to build dams on their land, contacted the Cree tribal council, of which the Nemaska band was a member, and pleaded for their help. The Cree tribal council brought suit against the government and hydro development agencies and won in a lower court. However, a higher court overturned the lower court's decision, claiming the right of eminent domain. The Quebec government claimed that power for six million Quebecois was more important than the right of six thousand Cree. However, in negotiations between the Cree tribal council and the government, it was decided that the Nemaska people had rights to their lands, and an agreement (the James Bay Agreement) was reached that the Nemaska could return and establish a new village in the area.

Fortunately, in the James Bay Agreement, the possibility of the Nemaska band returning to their area was laid out. Government funds were to be made available for the rebuilding of their village. There were two requirements: (1) within one year of the signing of the agreement, ninety band members had to formally pledge themselves to return to the area, and (2) within five years of the signing, at least ninety members must have established permanent residence in the new location. Within the year, ninety people formally pledged to return to the area.

The band chose the Institute of Cultural Affairs (ICA) Strategic Planning Process to determine how they would use the available funds to restore their village and plan their future. This method was developed by the Ecumenical Institute (headquartered in Chicago) as a way to help communities plan their future. Eventually some members separated from the Ecumenical Institute and organized themselves into the Institute of Cultural Affairs, with a large network in the United States and Canada.

Using the ICA Strategic Planning Process

The core purpose of the ICA Strategic Planning Process is to maximize the participation of people in taking responsibility for the societies, communities, and organizations in which they live and function. Using this process, consultants have evolved many useful group methods, such as getting participants to collect data, analyze information, and create vision. As it has evolved, the ICA Strategic Planning Process has been focused more on community development than on organization development or organizational change, although the principles work in private sector organizations as well.

The ICA Strategic Planning Process, which has been used with up to two hundred people, consists of the following steps (Spencer, 1989):

1. Focus on the question.
2. Map out a clear, practical vision.
3. Analyze the underlying contradictions (obstacles to achieving the vision).
4. Set the strategic directions (brainstorm for overcoming obstacles).
5. Design the systematic actions (strategies to achieve the vision).
6. Draw up an agreed-upon time line for implementation.

We will examine how the ICA Strategic Planning Process was used by consultants working with the Nemaska band's steering committee, which had been formed to plan the new village. The ICA Strategic Planning Process began with consultants working with this committee.

The steering committee's role was to set up a large group meeting that was to involve 100 people from the band plus 50 outside stakeholders who represented the key resources and skills needed to build the village. These areas included housing, architecture, education, health, and economic development. The steering committee's first task was to select a site for the new village. The Canadian government had been pressuring for a place that was accessible by road, but the band wanted a site on water that also faced the rising sun. According to project consultant Marcelene Anderson, after they chose a site on Champion Lake, all of the participants, including the consultants, cleared campsites so that they could work together in a large tent to create a vision and action plans. In contrast to the feelings of pain and despair the band had experienced at their removal from their land, as they engaged in clearing the land and putting up the tent, they felt a surge of hope that they were beginning to create their future.

Focus on the Question

The band's needs would "frame" the core question, an essential part of this five-day planning process. Thus, for the Nemaska, the question "What do we want for our new community?" was key. This question also included discerning what they wanted to carry over from the old community and what additional features they wanted to develop for their new community.

Map Out a Clear, Practical Vision

As with all future-planning methods, a clear, common vision of what participants would like to happen is key to success. Participants spent two days developing a clear vision, setting priorities, and evaluating the practicality of the vision.

A part of the practical vision generated by the band focused on physical facilities such as housing and utilities, as well as on ways to develop workable transportation, including an airstrip. Another part of the vision included services to the people of the band such as day care, community services, and offices to oversee these services. The band also envisioned the educational opportunities needed to provide training and skill development, education for children and adults, and human resource development. Finally, visioning focused on securing and expanding the economic base, including planning an arts-and-crafts center, exploring the development of tourist industries, and developing mink and other fur farming. After the vision was determined, the process then moved to the next step: discerning the underlying contradictions that get in the way of fulfilling the vision.

Analyze the Underlying Contradictions

According to this process, underlying contradictions are the blocks that prevent people from achieving their vision. The band spent approximately a day and a half brainstorming to uncover the blocks that could prevent them from achieving their vision. One block that emerged was their skill shortage: they did not know how to build the houses they would need to live in. Another was the fact that many of the band could only understand their own language. In addition, because they had been living in a fragmented way in two Cree villages in expectation of their land being flooded, it was difficult to pull people together to work for this process.

As they continued to probe, a fundamental block that emerged was the band's lack of trust: they doubted that the fifty resource people and the government would actually do what they said they would. Underlying this lack of trust was a lack of self-confidence and feelings of inadequacy when dealing with outside experts. The band's limited experience working and negotiating with outsiders, compounded by their culturally based reticence and shyness around outsiders, made them question their ability to be proactive and effectively manage the program.

This continual probing for contradictions, for the root causes underlying the blocks, is a unique feature of the ICA Strategic Planning Process. The probing of ideas to find out what causes a block and what underlies it continues until the participants uncover all of the possible contradictions. Many participants discover that, although they dislike a certain circumstance or behavior, in reality they often collude with the contradiction at some level through their current behavior. The most empowering question at this point is "How might we be contributing to this issue?" Once all the contradictions have been probed, participants can see them clearly; everything is out in the open. Then they can examine what contradictions they may be contributing to and can work to change their own individual stance. It is important to note that participants can change only their own behavior, not anyone else's.

We have found that when we ask this question as consultants, first there is a long silence, then a moment of truth. The change may be described as a movement from "them" to "us"—for example, from the band's idea that the government and resource people would betray or take advantage of them to the recognition that they had the power to achieve what they wanted. Once the barriers or contradictions to the vision are unearthed, participants can analyze the barriers and look deeper into the situation. They can look at what they want, then analyze any current actions that are in contradiction to getting the task done. Once the participants have this perception, they can see how to fix or overcome the obstacle.

Set the Strategic Directions

Strategic directions are the broad actions that deal with the underlying contradictions and find ways to circumvent them. Over the course of a day, participants first brainstorm about specific contradictions. They then go through all the brainstormed material, remove duplications, and sift out the best two or three ideas. The result is a list of strategic actions that can be taken.

It is important to note here the importance of having outside stakeholders present. The band realized, for example, that they needed the expertise of outside stakeholders to help them achieve some actions that they did not have the ability or expertise to achieve on their own. Another important realization, however, was that even though the band needed outside expertise, if they wanted to achieve their vision, they would have to manage the process, make the decisions, and take charge, which was a way of overcoming one of their major contradictions, their lack of self-esteem about their ability to handle interactions with outsiders.

Design the Systematic Actions

The next step in the ICA Strategic Planning Process is a tactical move: designing systematic actions to be taken. At this stage, participants ask what they have to do to "put wheels under the vision." During the visioning, the band had generated twenty-six different areas that needed addressing. Now, because of the tremendous number of tasks to be accomplished, the Nemaska organized themselves into task forces. Each group was responsible for developing specific action steps to work on the larger goals.

Draw Up an Agreed-Upon Time Line for Implementation

The next step is to draw up a time line for the specifics: Who does what? How long will it take? How often should the participants meet to keep the momentum going? A final, crucial question is: What does success look like?

During this part of the process, the band drew up a definite goal for each action on an implementation time line, for example, agreeing that homes would be built within a year. Today the Nemaska have built a flourishing, growing community with the limited funds provided by the government block grant. The only regret Chief George Wapachee has is that they did not have the requisite skills, at that time, to build their own homes.

Summary

The ICA Strategic Planning Process allows people to categorize, prioritize, and organize their own data, so everyone is involved, or, as Weisbord (1996) says, so that they are "touching the data." What could be just an exercise explodes into a whole-system approach that brings in all the stakeholders, not just a select few.

Also key to this process is that it is conducted over a period of five to seven days, with the actual time depending on a group's particular needs. What is important is that participants stay with the material over a period of time, which not only forces them to look deeper but also avoids the "quick fix" mentality. In the very process of participating in several days of intensive visioning, searching for contradictions, and offering solutions, participants begin to see possibilities and to take responsibility or ownership for the outcome of the process.

Consultants who use the ICA Strategic Planning Process believe that many blocks to projects or progress concern the self-concept of people in developing countries or in economically deprived communities in developed nations. This process is successful because it can empower people who previously assumed that they had no power, then moves them to take responsibility for creating the future they want or need. Lawrence Jimiken, a member of the Nemaska band, says that the most important aspect of this process for the band was that they believed in community-based planning, they created a plan, and they followed it.

Questions About ICA Strategic Planning Process

What happens to follow-up?
The usual approach is to have the steering committee coordinate the follow-up activities, with task force groups periodically reporting back on their progress. The Nemaska band used this process. In other situations, other structures, such as management structures, may already exist that would ensure that the initiative proceeds as planned.

Why has this process not been used more in the private sector?
We are aware of some use in the private sector, for example, by Texaco, Inc. in Nicaragua and by a few other companies, generally in work with small management groups. In the community development sector, it has been used with groups of up to two hundred people, both in the United States and overseas.

People who have used the ICA Strategic Planning Process in companies have continually commented about how helpful and useful it is. We agree and feel that this method is a simple but profound tool, especially in its probing of underlying contradictions. However, we also sense a reluctance in the private sector to adopt this method, possibly because of its association with community development. Although it seems fairly easy for ideas, methods, and strategies to move from the private to the public sector, the reverse occurs less often and, in this case, we wonder why.

Part Two Summary

Differences in Outcomes

As we talk to people all over the country, the comments about these methods from consultants and clients have been very positive. All things being equal, having the right purpose, including the right people in the room, and following the process as it is laid out help these methods work. It is important to recognize, however, that often the time frames for success are set five to twenty years into the future. Thus, in that sense, it is too early to tell about success. If we look at the example of the MBA program in Chapter Four, the curriculum was changed, some of the stovepipe departmentalism was changed, and new alliances with the business community were formed. Will this increase enrollment over the long haul? It is too early to tell. What can be said is that the school has made changes that are more in line with the needs of its customers and the external environment.

Using the ICA Strategic Planning Process, the Nemaska native Canadians explored and then overcame their inability to work proactively with outsiders and, in the process, built a beautiful new village. The Fund for the City of New York sponsored an event using Real Time Strategic Change, which was able to set up a system for managing a potential tuberculosis epidemic, reducing the incidence of tuberculosis by 15 percent. Using the Search Conference, a high-tech firm increased its market share and resolved some important internal issues.

"Did it work?" has another level. Important elements emerge from search conferences that carry back to the workplace. New relationships are formed at the conferences, old stereotypes are broken, and deeper understandings of the whole system and the environmental context become a shared data base for everyone. The conference takes down the boundaries between external and internal environments, between functions and levels. People learn new ways of working together.

In the same vein, we would like to offer a caution about putting change back into the workplace system. A member of the Sacramento (California) Teachers Association, who has run at least twenty conferences in school systems, recently said that follow-up and implementation depend on the new understandings and behaviors of the leadership. Or, to put it another way, once you have created the new wine of the future, you do not want to put it into an old wineskin (Matt. 9:17). The Emerys stress taking the culture created in the Search Conference and making sure that the culture change continues in the workplace, which may mean changing its bureaucratic structure.

At the beginning of Part Two, we described the process of recognizing, in retrospect, the power that a life planning workshop had on subsequent life and work. Picturing a desired or ideal future pulls you in that direction so that your actions, behaviors, and values are taking you there, whether you are aware of it or not. This approach is very different from our usual short-term mode, which expects instant results even if the goals are placed five or ten years in the future! Fortunately, when a system, community, or organization creates a common future, movement toward that future will begin to occur, often in subtle ways that are not always immediately identified. It is only in retrospect that we begin to recognize the influences of these desired futures.

As noted earlier, because of their future orientation, it is difficult to evaluate these methods. A consultant who has done a lot of work in schools and higher education systems made an interesting comment about gathering perceptual data on these change methods. The consultant asked people, in individual interviews, about the results of the conferences. The individuals had mixed views and were not sure about the results. Then the consultant brought together the whole system that had attended the event. Together, the group began to report all sorts of results, initiatives, and changes that had taken place and still were taking place. So the message here may be that you cannot measure systems change by collecting individual data; the system has to evaluate its own work.

We feel that these processes are powerful methods for generating energy and committed action toward building better futures for organizations and communities. Our hope is that as these processes are refined, more ways will be found to increase the number of stakeholders, especially for community settings, where more citizen involvement and interagency collaboration are essential for creating a better future. At a time when people across the country are fed up with government bureaucracy and question whether they, the citizens, have any influence, the methods discussed in this part have been found to be very helpful in building community and common cause between diverse interest groups; they help citizens to "take back" their communities.

Differences in the Methods

Having discussed differences in outcomes, we now turn to differences in the methods. What are the differences in these methods that may affect which one you choose? For the most part, these are differences in design, design flexibility, time involved, or numbers who can participate (see Part Two Summary Table).

Design Format

All four methods involve the system in planning the event, deciding who should attend, and planning follow-up. However, since the designs of the Search Conference, Future Search, and the ICA Strategic Planning Process are set and are not usually changed, the planning committee may not have much input in design. RTSC, on the other hand, tailors its design to each client issue and uses the

Part Two Summary Table.
Comparison: Large Group Methods for Creating the Future.

Method	Outcomes	Design Format	Decision-Making Process	Stakeholder Participation	Size of Event	Emphasis on Action Planning
The Search Conference	Agreements about future directions	Standard sequence	All equal	Yes for people within system boundary No for people outside system boundary	35 to 60	High
Future Search	Agreements about future directions	Standard sequence	All equal	Yes	Up to 100	Moderate
Real Time Strategic Change	Agreements about future directions	Variable sequence Standard modules	Consultative	Yes	Up to 2,400	High
ICA Strategic Planning Process	Agreements about future directions	Standard sequence	All equal	Yes, as appropriate	50 to 200	High

planning group to test-run the design. Clients plan jointly with the consultants, working for consensus on the design. The consultants are experts on designing. The clients are experts on their system, their culture, and how people are likely to react. Both types of expertise are necessary for successful designs.

Size of Event

How many people can be invited? That depends on which method is chosen. Merrelyn Emery prefers to work with about 35 people, but simultaneous events or multisearches are possible when more participants are wanted. We note that some Americans are doing Search Conferences with up to 60 people. Future Search (Weisbord and Janoff, 1995) prefers 75 people but numbers from 80 to 150 are also successfully handled as are simultaneous conferences. The latter, of course, create an additional step whose outcomes need to be integrated. This can be done by merging themes from skits across all the conferences and then doing action planning with the larger total group.

RTSC is the most flexible about numbers. This method asks the planning committee to determine what numbers are needed to achieve a critical mass that will, in fact, change the organization in real time. The event is then planned for that number, which may range from 100 to thousands.

Stakeholder Participation

Stakeholders are involved differently across these methods. Future Search and the ICA Strategic Planning Process invite them as equal participants. Stakeholder input is represented by those who are present. The Search Conference prefers to gather stakeholder information in advance, sometimes as a pre-event assignment. The rule of thumb is to have only those people present at the conference who can be responsible later for outcomes, in other words, members of the organization or system. RTSC may invite stakeholders but, just as often, they are invited in for only part of the event. They are often asked to make short presentations and respond to queries. You can hear a pin drop when a customer who has rejected the company comes in to tell the participants what the experience of dealing with the company was like and why it did not make the sale!

Time

Finally, the typical length of these interventions is different. Both Future Search and the Search Conference are typically two-day events, lasting eighteen hours over two nights (an afternoon, a whole day, and a morning). RTSC events can be one, two, or three days long, depending on the objectives and what needs to happen in the design. These events can also be serial—for example, a one-day orienting event followed several weeks later by a two-day decision-making event. ICA events are the longest because they try to complete a whole process—from orientation, through planning, to action assignments—at one time. Their events are often five to seven days in length.

Design Format and Action Planning

Most of these methods have fairly standard preplanned designs. The value here is that the designs have been thoroughly tested in hundreds of situations. The exception is RTSC, which creates a new design for each new client setting, often using well-tested standard modules. All of the methods are concerned about action planning. The differences are in how much time is set aside for action planning in the overall design.

Choosing a Method

Let's imagine that your organization needs to do some significant future planning. You have heard about these methods and think that they are exciting. You would like to suggest using one of them but are uncertain which one to propose. Of course, these kinds of decisions are not simple and linear. Some factors are rational; however, others are not, like who the consultants and clients are and how the chemistry works between them.

One way to begin is by establishing an overall educational process with the top decision makers. People who have not experienced these large group events often fear chaos. Videotapes of actual events and short readings from some of the material listed in the Appendix can help you to put together an educational program that will orient people to what is possible and what an event might be like.

Several key factors may push you in the direction of one method or another. The first is the nature of power and control in the organization or community with which you are involved. Power is dispersed in communities and in some types of organizations, for example, educational institutions. In these settings, in order to plan for the future and take action, a coalescence of power needs to take place. Future Search, the ICA Strategic Planning Process, and the Search Conference all give everyone a vote in co-creating the future. This allows people to find common ground that they share and move ahead.

On the other hand, many organizations have managements that see themselves as charged with leadership and as setting the strategic direction for the future. At the same time, they know that they need others to be involved and to have a voice in setting the strategic direction. Real Time Strategic Change allows management to craft a vision and to try it out and get feedback from the organization before it is cast in stone. This creates an interactive, reciprocal process in which the members of the organization can influence management and become committed to and aligned with the organization's future goals. Another key factor may be the size of the group that needs to be present to attain a critical mass. As we have indicated, if the numbers are very big, only RTSC can handle them in one event.

If a strong probability exists that the new vision of the future will entail some changes in organizational structure and you foresee the possibility of a participative redesign process, you may want to look over the interventions in Part Three of this book. Many redesign processes begin with work on the organization's vision.

Part Three

The Methods
Work Design

Years ago, when I (Billie) was helping run a family marine transportation business in Ecuador, I stumbled on an interesting fact: the work force often has a far better sense than management of how to organize and structure work.

Usually, the ship had a very informal and egalitarian atmosphere, more like that of an extended family, in spite of differences in education and skill. One year we purchased expensive and, I thought, attractive uniforms for the tanker's crew and officers. We thought they would help to establish a sense of hierarchy and clearer roles and responsibilities among the officers and crew. The crew seemed pleased with the uniforms; however, as we journeyed up the Pacific Coast to the Panama Canal, I noticed that they were not wearing them. When I asked why, they responded, "We don't need them now." I thought that perhaps they just wanted to keep the uniforms clean.

In the meantime, the usual informal atmosphere predominated. The captain thought nothing, during his off hours, of going down and relieving the oiler. Everyone joined in for certain tasks such as painting and swabbing the decks. Often, it was impossible to tell who were the officers and who were the crew, because they all were in jeans and T-shirts, helping out where they could be useful.

Imagine my surprise the morning we arrived at the entrance to the Panama Canal, where the Panama Canal pilot comes on board. Everyone was standing at attention, in place, and in uniform! Overnight, we had gone from an egalitarian, informal system to a hierarchical, formal one. As we moved through the canal, orders were called out and repeated in the best British naval tradition. I could not believe my eyes and ears! As soon as we exited the Panama Canal, the uniforms came off and we were relaxed and informal again—until we arrived at Aruba, where the hierarchical structure was put in place once more.

What I learned then, and what I have seen many times since, was that our employees knew how to structure and organize themselves according to the requirements of the task. Only later, when I read *Three Studies in Management* (Scott and Lynton, 1952), the British coal mine study that gave birth to Socio-Technical Systems design concepts, did I understand my experience. On the ship, however, I had no fancy words or concepts to describe what I was seeing. It worked, and I had the good sense not to interfere!

The Pressure to Change

The employees on the ship had designed their own structural changes to fit the requirements of the task. Most employees, however, are understandably suspicious when they hear the words *restructure* or *redesign*. And no wonder, since redesign and restructure are processes that often happen arbitrarily, with little employee influence or involvement.

At the same time, today's business environment forces companies to confront a constant stream of tough questions about the future: What business are we in? Where is our market and how has it changed? Who is and who will be our competition? How do our costs compare to those of our competition? Questions like these force management to consider new directions.

Two Methods of Business Redesign

The two methods currently most used to change the way businesses are structured are reengineering (Hammer and Champy, 1993) and Socio-Technical Systems (Pasmore, 1994). Reengineering focuses on finding better ways to organize and structure key business processes; remove duplication and unnecessary steps, policies, and procedures; and use information technology to improve work processing. The reengineering analysis is usually performed by a specially appointed task force that represents the company's internal expertise with the help of outside consultants. The task force makes recommendations for change in order to structure processes and reduce costs.

Socio-Technical Systems (STS) is a method created in the 1950s in England by Eric Trist and Fred Emery (see Chapter Two for more details) that became widely used in the United States in the 1980s. STS design is a process of analyzing and fitting together the social system (people's skills, knowledge, experience, and relationship networks) and the technical system (the technical process by which the work gets done) to maximize both productivity and a positive work environment. Like reengineering, however, the analyses and recommendations for change were performed by a representative group of workers and management, the design team, who often took a year to complete their work. During this time, the members of the organization who were not participating were left in the dark to wonder and grow suspicious about how these changes might affect them. As a result, even excellent suggestions for change had to be "sold" to the rest of the organization, which was often resistant to change.

In the end, the problems of acceptance and commitment to

change by the work force are similar for STS design and reengineering, even though the processes are different.

Whole-System Participatory Approaches to Redesign

The tanker crew in the story at the beginning of this introduction had a keen sense of how they needed to organize to get work done. More recently, the practitioners of STS design represented in the following chapters have recognized the problems created by traditional practice and have begun to employ large group methods to involve the whole system in the redesign effort. Led by Dick Axelrod, whose Conference Model® was the first of these large-scale redesign processes (see Chapter Seven), Bill Pasmore, Gary Frank, and Al Fitz created Fast Cycle Full Participation Work Design, using large group meetings (see Chapter Eight). Most recently, Paul Tolchinsky joined Kathleen Dannemiller to create Real Time Work Design (see Chapter Nine). All three are variations of STS using large group methods to increase participation and reduce the time to implementation. Part Three Figure graphically represents the important characteristics of all the work design methods.

Over the years, Fred Emery, one of the creators of Socio-Technical Systems design, grew frustrated with traditional STS practice and endorsed a new participative process called Participative Design (see Chapter Ten). Rather than beginning at the top of the organization, this process begins by allowing those who do the core work of the organization to design and control their work guided by specific design principles. Then the rest of the organization is redesigned to support the core work process. In this sense, it can be described as a bottom-up rather than a top-down process.

Part Three Figure. Large Group Methods for Work Design.

THE CONFERENCE MODEL®
Dick and Emily Axelrod

- System-Wide Preconference Education
- Design Process in Five Conferences
  ◊ Vision
  ◊ Customer
  ◊ Technical
  ◊ Design
  ◊ Implementation
- Three+ Weeks Between Conferences
- 2+ Days for Each Conference
- Data Assist Teams Work Between Meetings to Involve Larger Organization
- 80+ Participants, Parallel Conferences for Larger Groups

FAST CYCLE FULL PARTICIPATION WORK DESIGN
Pasmore, Fitz, and Frank

- Orientation Events Educate and Include Everyone
- Five Meetings
  ◊ Future Search (2 Days)
  ◊ Meeting External Expectations (1 Day)
  ◊ Work Systems Analysis (2 to 3 Days)
  ◊ Work Life Analysis (1 Day)
  ◊ New Design and Implementation (4+ Days)
- Up to 120 Attend Meetings
- Parallel Design of Support Process Changes
- 1/3 of System Participation Goal
- Design Ratification Events Include Everyone

REAL TIME WORK DESIGN
Dannemiller and Tolchinsky

- Whole System Present at Launch and Implementation
- 50 to 2,400 Participants
- Process, Design, Deep Dive Conferences Representative
- 1-Day Conferences on Key Administrative Support Issues
- Design Team Manages Process and Does Micro-Work
- Implementation Team Oversees Mini-Conferences

PARTICIPATIVE DESIGN
Fred and Merrelyn Emery

- Bottom-Up Process
- Company-Wide Education Is First Step
- Management Sets Minimum Critical Specifications
- Basic Principle: Each Level Coordinates and Controls Its Own Work
- Each Unit Designs Its Own Work
- Six Design Principles Used to Redesign Work
- Multiskilling Is the Norm

Chapter Seven

The Conference Model®

Having experienced some of the dysfunctional aspects of traditional reengineering and Socio-Technical Systems design, Dick and Emily Axelrod, deciding that there had to be a better way, developed the Conference Model®, which compresses design time and increases commitment to design outcomes by involving as many people as possible from the start in a series of two- or three-day conferences over four to five months (Axelrod, 1992).

To develop the Conference Model®, the Axelrods use a visioning conference based on the Future Search Conference to start the redesign process, then follow it with four other conferences. Although variations in the format exist, the standard approach is a series of five conferences:

1. The first conference is a Visioning Conference, in which those who participate develop a vision of what they would like the organization to be in the future.

2. The second conference is a Customer Conference. Here the participants develop an understanding of both internal and external customer requirements. These requirements, and the vision, contribute to the design criteria.

3. In the third conference, the Technical Conference, current work flow is studied to highlight problems and variances that occur as work, services, and people flow through the system. Because participants have a vision of the future, they can look at the current work flow based on this vision, not simply on what can be "fixed."

4. The fourth conference is the Design Conference. Information developed in the previous conferences is used to create a new design for work.

5. The final conference is an Implementation Conference (more than one may be held, if needed). At the implementation conference or conferences, each unit performs the final detailed work on its own structure; identifies teams, roles, and responsibilities; sets goals and new behaviors required; and establishes a time frame for implementation.

Getting Everyone Involved: The Data Assist Team

The conferences are held about a month apart, with eighty to ninety people attending each conference. A core group of about a third of the conference attends all conferences and as many employees as possible will attend at least one conference. A critical factor for success is the continued involvement and commitment of employees who cannot attend every conference. These employees will be kept informed by and involved through the *data assist team*.

The data assist team forms the communication channel with the whole system between conferences. Members of this team, who are also part of the design team, attend all conferences and are assigned to the data assist team for the duration of the Conference Model® process. In some cases, they are relieved from their everyday duties and focus solely on their duties for the data assist team. This interesting innovation not only increases communication with the larger system but also involves those employees who have not yet attended or cannot attend a conference.

Members of the data assist team receive training in data synthesis, presentation skills, and techniques for enhancing group participation. Their tasks are to:

• Take the data from each conference
• Synthesize that information

- Facilitate a "walk-through" with groups of twenty to thirty employees who could not attend the previous conference

At these walk-throughs, which are two- to four-hour meetings describing the conference and the results, videos of the conference are often used to show people what happened. This method keeps employees in the loop and lets them know what is going on. In addition, people who have used the Conference Model® report that seeing videos of peers interacting and participating generates significant interest and energy about the conference process.

Walk-through meetings go beyond merely rehashing what happened at the conference; they become "mini-conferences" in and of themselves. Employees' ideas and opinions are solicited about the previous conference and then are forwarded as input for the next conference. The Conference Model® employs elements such as an open structure, deliberate communication, and full inside stakeholder involvement that are often missing in redesign efforts that operate as closed systems until the plan is announced.

Another key to the Conference Model® is the presence of outside stakeholders. In traditional redesign efforts, stakeholders are usually interviewed or surveyed. However, experience with the Conference Model® suggests that the physical, participative presence of these stakeholders, for example, customers and suppliers, provides more and better information than even the most sophisticated survey data. Employees repeatedly report the importance of hearing customers and suppliers talk about their business, the pressures they are under, how their business is changing, and what the company can do to help them. Customers report how valuable it is to be invited to the conferences, to meet the employees and understand their hopes and constraints, and to be part of the process to improve the whole. Connecting the system in this interactive way generates new understanding and new partnerships.

This approach differs radically from the usual restructure or redesign process, whether it is performed by consultants, senior management, or a small group of representative employees who are familiar with the work flow. The Conference Model's® steps are not unique: reengineering and traditional Socio-Technical design all take these analytic steps. What is unique is the direct involvement of outside stakeholders, senior management, employees, and even board members.

The Conference Model® has been applied in a variety of organizations—airlines, financial institutions, and health care systems, to name a few—and those who use it find it to be quite flexible in how the series of conferences are applied. In several instances, for example, the customer and vision conferences have been successfully combined. In another instance, since work had been done on the vision and work-flow analysis, the conference focused on designing and implementing self-managing teams. Some organizations are using individual conferences to work through very specific issues such as understanding a core process or customer-supplier relationships.

A Case Study: Mercy Healthcare

The many and rapid changes occurring in the health care field today require a whole realignment of hospital systems. In Sacramento, California, Mercy Healthcare, which consists of five hospitals, decided to use the Conference Model® as part of their 1995 effort to become a regional health care network. First, we will look at the use of the Conference Model® at Mercy Healthcare; then we will reflect on some of the questions and implications of this approach.

Background

Mercy Healthcare set up a steering committee of about thirty people to look at alternatives for organizational design. The steering committee consisted of two physicians plus management representatives from the five hospitals. The committee members had benchmarked approaches taken by different hospitals and had decided not to use the reengineering, department-by-department approach that currently was being implemented by other hospitals. Instead, the committee chose the Conference Model®. In the opening talk by Mercy Healthcare's CEO, Sister Bridget McCarthy, it was clear that this approach touched the core values of the Sisters of Mercy. They saw this method as helping to identify process issues at all levels and locations in the organization, to generate more creative ideas, and to allow for greater understanding of and preparation for change. They planned to involve three thousand people, including employees, physicians, patients, and suppliers. Mercy Healthcare's use of the Conference Model® had some unique elements:

- Representatives participated from all five hospitals.
- Four simultaneous conferences were held for the visioning-customer and technical conferences.
- One data assist team, made up of four employees helped by members of the steering committee, integrated the data from each of the conferences and shared information with over three thousand employees by creating mini-conferences.
- Two doctors who attended the meetings took on the responsibility of communicating with the other physicians who could not attend the conferences about the purposes and outcomes of each conference. They used the videos to help other physicians experience what had happened at the conference.
- Two key processes were selected for analysis and redesign: (1) patient access and flow and (2) service care delivery.
- In line with their spiritual orientation, each conference began with a period of centering and reflection.

The Visioning-Customer Conference

As people arrived at and chatted before the visioning-customer conference (the two were combined at Mercy), it was clear that they had both concerns and hopes. People were pleased at the opportunity to be a part of the process. However, they also brought with them their own agendas and concerns.

Sister Bridget opened the visioning-customer conference by discussing the organization's three goals: (1) to reduce expenses by thirty to thirty-five million dollars by 1997, (2) to create meaningful work and improve satisfaction among the stakeholders, and (3) to enhance clinical outcomes by integrating processes and more effectively coordinating care. She also openly acknowledged the pain that many of these changes could cause. In all likelihood, there would be fewer jobs. However, the hard news about the bottom line was softened by Sister Bridget's commitment to look for other jobs for people whose positions were cut as well as to offer retraining when possible. The open communication style of the Conference Model® allowed the reality to be stated and the resulting tension acknowledged, while also allowing the organization to honor its value of commitment to the well-being not only of its patients but also of its employees.

After this introduction, the visioning-customer conference proceeded by putting patients, doctors, and payers into "fishbowls." In this method, the focus group sits in the middle of the room surrounded by the other conference participants, who listen to the conversation taking place "in the fishbowl." The people in the fishbowl usually talk about their experiences and concerns as stakeholders. The fishbowl format illustrated the complexity of balancing the needs of such a diverse group of stakeholders. It also gave the participant observers some insight into other perspectives as well as underlining the complexity of those perspectives. Other results of this part of the conference were a better understanding of the organization's history and current situation and recognition of the kind of future organization the participants wished to create.

The Technical Conference

The technical conference is always a pivotal one because this is the first time many employees are able to see the whole. One of the things we know about change is that you cannot fix just part of a system. You have to work on and maximize the whole so that, as employees see the whole process flow, their perspective changes. They start to own the whole system, not just their little bit of turf, confirming Marvin Weisbord's observation that unless you understand how the whole system works, you can't control it (Weisbord, personal communication, 1992). This understanding is critical to change. The more that people understand it, the better their chances are of improving it.

At the Mercy Healthcare conference, the second day opened with Sister Bridget's introduction to the next few days. She invited participants "not to be constrained by existing systems. Rather create your own structures to sustain life and foster growth." She also reiterated the need to get rid of worn-out rules and outmoded procedures.

Over 350 people attended this meeting in four simultaneous groups. Again, the task was to examine two key processes: (1) access and flow and (2) service care delivery. The groups analyzed the processes to determine the major problems, variances, breakdowns, and redundancies that occurred. The approach was to create a large process map on the wall indicating the major phases in the flow. Post-it Notes were then placed on each phase, and participants described the activities that occur within that phase.

The participants then engaged in a fun and revealing exercise of what happens to patients as they move through the system. All the participants sat in their respective stakeholder groups. An actual patient, one of the stakeholders attending the conference, was given a patient diagnosis scenario. As she was "treated" by the system, she moved through the different service areas (admissions, testing, X-ray, and so forth). Post-it Notes were placed on her dress, indicating what had been done to her in each area and how long she had had to wait.

As different tables reported their analysis of this process, it was clear how many redundant, duplicative, and unnecessary procedures were taking place. For example, a minor test that could be done quickly at the patient's bedside was sent to the laboratory, primarily because the laboratory could then charge for the work. This procedure was driven not by efficiency or patient service but by financial considerations.

The Design Conference

The design conference that followed was done in two groups, each focusing on one of the key processes selected. The purpose was to develop a macro-design, which would then become a template from which units across the region would customize and implement, given differences in patient services.

On the second day of the design conference, the session started in one large group. As a total community, the participants generated a giant mind map (Buzan, 1976), calling out ideas and insights generated from their previous work—the elements that needed to be incorporated into the new design. The groups then separated into different rooms, and each group worked on redesign for its key process. Periodically, general community sessions were held in which the groups shared their thinking to that point and received feedback from the other groups.

The Implementation Conference

After board approval of the generic design (template) was obtained and financial analysis of the new design was worked out, the implementation conference could go forward. Five teams, set up as part of the implementation strategy, were made responsible for dealing with the policy and procedural issues associated with redesign, for example, job descriptions and how people would make the transition into new jobs. This included information systems, because all of these changes had to be coordinated with and integrated into the information systems framework.

The hoped-for outcomes—reduced costs and less duplication,

improved patient care, increased efficiency, and more job satisfaction—would result from giving people:

- More responsibility
- More meaningful work
- More meaningful interaction with patients
- Less bureaucracy
- More decision making at the level where it needs to occur
- Increased staff empowerment
- Better working relationships between groups

Why This Method Works: Congruence with Values

One reason the Conference Model® worked so well at Mercy Healthcare was the model's congruence with Mercy's own value system—that is, the recognition that high participation in the change process would help in the contribution of information, new ideas, and the acceptance and implementation of change.

A steering committee or planning group needs to consider some key ideas before selecting an approach to managing change:

- What are our values?
- Does this approach fit our value system?
- Do we believe that by involving a number of stakeholders and employees, the quality of the ideas and the acceptance of change will be greatly enhanced?

As Mercy Healthcare's experience confirmed, one value that people consistently need is honesty. For example, Mercy Healthcare needed to cut costs, and that reality was presented honestly and up front. All of the stakeholders were fully informed and thus had a chance to begin to find solutions for themselves. If management had not valued being honest with the employees, the layoffs would have come anyway, and people would have been left with significantly fewer options for themselves or for changing the underlying work systems. Avoiding pain in the short term would have led to more costs and more pain in the long run.

Questions About the Conference Model®

What is the role of leadership in the Conference Model®?
The leadership has to be willing to find a workable balance. The process cannot merely be blessed by the leadership or delegated to committees. It needs the leadership's active participation, which demonstrates their commitment to the change process. As one participant noted, the Conference Model® is an "on-the-job exercise in learning how to let go—without abdicating."

Does this methodology generate a detailed design?
Detailed designs are usually worked out in the implementation phase. However, people using this method note that even before the design conference is complete, participants are beginning to act differently in relationship to each other and their respective departments. This was confirmed in conversation with Barbara Feldman, from Corning, Inc., and Gary Hochman, from the Hewlett-Packard Company, both of whom have extensive experience with this method. Even before the design and implementation conferences take place, people have left the technical conference knowing what they need to do differently, and they have built the relationships at the conference to jointly begin to make these changes happen.

The same behavior was reported by Don Krebs, the senior organization development consultant at the Boeing Company for the 777 start-up, mentioned in Chapter Four. Managers will often run a two-hour, two-hundred-person meeting in which critical workflow issues are examined and discussed. Once it is clear just where the "glitches" are, participants do not need to spend endless hours devising minutely detailed action plans. Instead, Krebs affirms, "People know what they need to do, and they do it" (Dallas Conference, 1995).

Will people have a vested interest in maintaining their own job and refuse to make any changes that jeopardize that job?
This objection always comes up any time large-scale structural change is mentioned. Will people risk participating when it is clear that these decisions may very well cause them to lose their job? In our observations of the Conference Model® at work as well as in conversations with consultants and participants, we can say that the answer is yes. People prefer to have an influence on the process rather than having change imposed upon them. People do tackle the tough questions. How? We believe that a definite shift takes place in these meetings.

As people arrive and begin to interact, it is clear that they bring along their own individual concerns and the agenda of their stakeholder group. Toward the end of the first conference, however, we see a noticeable shift from "me" to "we." Something inherent in the sharing of different perspectives leads participants to envision a larger, more complete picture and to discover how much they have in common. The focus shifts from "How can I get my agenda met?" to a sense of shared purpose.

We believe that a number of factors generate this shift. One factor is having participants sit in mixed groups. In these groups, people share their perceptions and frustrations and contribute to a new view. Another factor is that many of the opening exercises, such as history charts and mind maps, put the organization in the context of the larger society; individual issues are modified, suspended, or even dropped in favor of contemplating the whole.

In addition, the presence of customers (or patients, in Mercy Healthcare's case) helps participants to focus on those they ultimately serve. Providing quality goods and services to customers is a source of meaning and purpose. In organizations in which daily business activities are divorced from this sense of meaning, work can become merely a paid chore. It is difficult to understand why so many organizations have designed themselves in a way that allows few people to have the chance to interact with customers.

*What is the emotional process for participants in the Conference Model®
as they see and understand the whole?*
Participating in the Conference Model® is rather like riding a roller coaster. The visioning-customer conference is usually energizing and "a high" because we often disagree less about the ideal future than about how to get there. The technical conference is insightful, but also overwhelming, as everyone realizes how much needs to be done. The design and implementation conferences are just plain hard work and can be frustrating as well. In making the decision to go this route, leadership needs to be aware of the ups and downs of the roller coaster ride. They also need to remember that it takes courage and determination to stay with it. At the same time, we would encourage people, as much as they can, to enjoy the ride. It is exhilarating, and sometimes scary, but it always is worth it. From all reports, it works, if the process is followed with integrity.

*How much ownership do employees who have not attended the confer-
ences have in the new design?*
The data assist teams make every effort to involve and inform employees. In a survey done in the Mercy Healthcare system, only 15 percent felt that they had not been sufficiently informed and that they had had little influence. That is not too bad a record.

*The Conference Model® seems to require a large investment of time.
How is this justified?*
People have reported to us that managers often become impatient and want to give the tasks to a small group, so that they can "get on with it." This does not mean that a smaller group is never appropri-ate—it may well be. But the work, as it progresses, needs to be shared constantly with the system to get feedback and to discover implications.

It is also important to remember that the Conference Model® actually requires *much less time* than traditional approaches, which can take two years or more. The implementation phase happens much more quickly because people have been part of creating the plan. They have better ownership and commitment to making it work, and far less resistance.

Are customers and suppliers willing to give up the time to come to these conferences?
In all the methods in this book that involve external stakeholders, people have reported how honored these stakeholders are to be included in the process and how responsive they are in terms of their support and their willingness to assist the organization in its goals.

Is all the work done in a large group format?
Not necessarily, especially for design details. Smaller groups could work on a design element; however, they always need to report back to the larger group and get feedback, additional suggestions, and confirmation.

Chapter Eight

Fast Cycle Full Participation Work Design

Bill Pasmore, a professor at the Weatherhead School of Management at Case Western Reserve in Cleveland, Ohio, took the lead in getting practitioners who were doing traditional Socio-Technical Systems (STS) design together in an annual meeting to talk about their work and think about what they were learning in their practice. As large group methods developed in the 1980s and as the corporate environment became more and more demanding of organizational responsiveness, Pasmore, Gary Frank, Al Fitz, and Mary Pasmore integrated these methods with traditional STS practice to create Fast Cycle Full Participation Work Design (FCFP).

The Six Key Processes of the Structure

This method does some of the work in large group meetings and some in smaller groupings in between large group events. Six key processes often occur at large group meetings that are one to three days long:

1. Orientation
2. Search Conference
3. Stakeholder expectations
4. Technical work system analysis
5. Work life analysis
6. New design and implementation

Orientation

When an organization signs up for a redesign, everyone needs to know what is going to happen, what the goals are, and how they can be involved. Orientations can be large group meetings or can be held in smaller forums. Either way, people get information, a chance to talk about it, and the opportunity to ask questions about the process and their role in it. The goal is to involve everyone in the organization in the orientation.

An important aspect of orientation is education about what participative work is like, what it expects of people, and what the rewards and stresses may be. In many bureaucratic organizations where people are socialized into being rather passive and authority-dependent, this is the first step in alerting people to the new culture that will be required to sustain redesign and the new behaviors that will be required of them.

At Nabisco, for example, at the beginning of a FCFP project to redesign a major manufacturing plant, the orientation occurred in groups of about seventy-five over a three-week period. The two-hour sessions were opened by union and management, who introduced the project and their hopes and expectations for it. After the business case for change was presented, everyone participated in a work redesign simulation. (It is possible to use any one of a number of these simulations.) They begin with enacting a traditional one-person, one-job production line controlled by a supervisor. Then, participants are asked to redesign the work for better efficiency and working conditions. Finally, the new designs are run and evaluated. These simulations are very involving, are fun, and usually produce good learning. After this, the redesign process and schedule was rolled out, and an opportunity was provided for questions and answers. Notice that the process used in the orientation was typical of work design events.

The Search Conference

FCFP uses a modified version of Future Search, which they call the

"Search Conference." This two-day, up to 120 person event, begins with global trends, predicts what the future will bring the organization as a result of these trends, reviews the personal and organizational milestones of the past, projects a desirable future, and applies all of these learnings to a first cut at design ideas for the new organization. Each Search Conference is composed of representatives of the whole system to be redesigned. In all of the events that are not targeted to involve the entire organization, critical mass is seen as consisting of about one third of the organization. In a 900-employee plant, for example, three Search Conferences of 100 people each would be run. The design for the Search has flexibility. Using the general pattern described in Chapter Four, some changes will be made in response to the specific situation. If union-management relations are strained, for example, the "prouds and sorries" activity may be included. Interestingly, rather than converging the themes from the skits about the future, Pasmore, Fitz, and Frank prefer to allow the thirty or forty "visions" to stand as they are, representing the many ideas present about a better organization. After the Search Conference is over, the process of communicating to the other two thirds of the organization begins. In FCFP, the planning committee decides how people will be kept up-to-date on the results of the various events. The strategy is to use any and all media that make sense in that situation. This can include meetings, E-mail, voice mail, the company newsletter, videotapes of the events, dedicated communication groups that hold meetings, and whatever other creative solutions they can generate.

Stakeholder Expectations

If a new organizational structure is to be effective, it has to improve both the internal technical work system and the interactions of the organization with the environment. A one-day meeting, which can range from modest in size to several hundred, is held with all the external stakeholders who place demands on the organization. This includes groups such as customers, suppliers, competitors, and regulators. It can also include internal stakeholders such as corporate human resources, information systems, and the quality organization.

The task of this meeting in table groups of stakeholders and organization members is to interview the stakeholders and find out about their current and future expectations of the organization and the strengths and weaknesses of their current relationship with the company. This opens up a dialogue that focuses the members of the organization on listening carefully to the stakeholders, putting themselves in the stakeholders' shoes, and understanding what they want and need.

Disconnects often occur—for example, between what the central engineering department that provides new technology thinks a plant needs and what the plant wants. At one company, a long history of poor and sometimes acrimonious relationships shifted when, as a result of the dialogue at this event, a technology committee that included key players from both the plant and corporate headquarters was set up to meet quarterly. The purpose was to educate everyone about new technologies that were available and to discuss their merits as well as how changes could be made with minimum disruption.

At the end of an analysis of stakeholder views, the group generates design ideas for the new organization and brainstorms better ways to meet stakeholder requirements.

Technical Work System Analysis

The two- or three-day meeting to do the technical work system analysis involves the people who are the experts, that is, those who actually do the work as well as others in the organization who are internal stakeholders. Typically, from 60 to 120 people are involved in each meeting. The content of these meetings varies depending on whether routine or nonroutine work systems are being analyzed. Manufacturing plants are examples of locations where routine work is done, with predictable steps in series to produce the product. Some service delivery is also predictable, for example, the service delivered by an airplane cabin crew or the registration process for classes at a university. Nonroutine work occurs when unpredictable decision-making processes take place, as when a new product or marketing strategy is created.

Routine work systems use the traditional STS process of laying out the steps in the work flow. This is a critical and sometimes difficult step. Participants from each product line work very hard to be sure that they have laid out each step in the process map accurately. The participants then list the "variances" or errors that can occur in the process that make it less efficient or that interfere with quality. Looking over these lists, they pick the key variances, the ones that contribute the most to loss of quality and efficiency, and suggest ways to eliminate these variances.

In the traditional STS design process, this is crucial work that is done to a very fine level of analysis, often taking weeks or months. How can it be done in two or three days with such a large group? Bill Pasmore believes that there are tradeoffs. The large numbers at the technical analysis make identifying the key variances much more probable. Selecting the right variances is crucial to redesign success. A more finely tuned analysis can be carried out by a separate team in follow-up meetings after the event. This is especially true with alternative solutions to reduce variances. Breakthrough solutions are hard to get in large, diverse groups. Smaller groups with more depth of knowledge and more time to let ideas percolate are often needed.

Nonroutine work, work that is different every time it is performed, is examined for the decision-making process and flow and for knowledge management processes. Patterns of deliberations are identified. Key deliberations that create successes or failures for the organization are selected and variances identified. The implications of these analyses for the design of the organization are explored and a new design selected. At the Goodyear Tire and Rubber Company, new customer-focused research and development teams were created. At Polaroid Corporation, large weekly meetings were replaced with smaller, focused discussions of technical opportunities.

Work Life Analysis

Satisfying human needs is central to STS design's dual concern for products and people. What kind of work environment with what kinds of jobs will allow people to feel that they are engaged in meaningful work? How do structures provide satisfying human interaction on the job? What kind of climate will provide respect for each person and her or his contributions? These are some of the questions that this analysis addresses in a one-day meeting with representatives of the whole system in the room. The outcome is identification of the best and worst jobs in the present and the characteristics that are desirable in jobs. Then ideas are generated about how to create jobs in the newly designed organization, including what the organization wants to keep, change, or create. Someone might say, for example, "I'd like to repair my own equipment. I'm tired of standing around waiting for Maintenance. Why can't I be certified to do it?" Or a group might decide that they want more voice in working conditions and governance, even in how they are compensated.

New Design and Implementation

Finally, it is time to create the new design for the organization. At the beginning of the two-day design event, the future visions from the Search Conference are revisited. Individuals in groups imagine a future organization that they share with others and identify common themes. Next, they identify the core work of the organization and set the boundaries. They then define the support work that is needed to support the core. Finally, they define the administrative work that is required. This creates the design for the new organization.

This process sets out the macro-design for the organization. Detailed implementation work is then needed in the new units to establish jobs, roles, and responsibilities. Implementation occurs in the work units where, using a method similar to Emery's Participative Design, each unit works out its own functioning in a process that Pasmore, Fitz, and Frank call micro-design. Thus, everyone is involved in making the design a reality.

Questions About Fast Cycle Full Participation Work Design

How flexible is this design?
The central elements of the way FCFP operates have been given above. Each input is important to the final design, but considerable flexibility exists, based on the client's needs and the situation. In one project, for example, the plant manager wanted everyone in the plant to participate in the final design meeting, so two large meetings were held and the designs were integrated. With other projects, a representative sample of the larger organization would do that work.

What about other systems that can affect the success of a new design?
One bête noir in traditional STS work has been when a successful design process has difficulties at the implementation stage because the other organizational control systems such as the pay system or the performance appraisal system does not reinforce the new design and climate, but rather sabotages it. Pasmore and his associates are collaborating with Sibson & Company, a compensation consulting firm, in working at thirty-one Levi Strauss and Company sites and have created a parallel but separate process to start thinking about the structure of the pay system from the very beginning of the project. The intention is that when the new design is ready for implementation, a congruent pay system will also be ready.

How much time is saved by using this method?
Comparing FCFP with traditional STS methods that often take two years or more from start to full implementation, this method can save a great deal of time. The six meetings can be run in about six months, one per month. When 100 percent of the system is

involved, it may take longer, because of the need to keep the plant or business open and functioning. As part of the planning, clients determine when it is important to involve everyone and when a diagonal slice of the organization will do.

The meetings, however, are not the whole story. First, the system must get ready for the redesign project. In situations with a union, this involves working through issues with the union in advance so that both groups sponsor the project. This can take time when relationships are strained. Implementation is the other unknown on the time line. If the process is very complex as, for example, it may be in continuous process plants like refineries, or if a plant has several product lines that are all in redesign, the implementation schedule will take longer than in simpler settings. In addition, what happens to the company in its environment can affect the implementation process. Experienced practitioners can give good estimates, but more often, client needs determine the total time.

What are the differences in doing work design between nonroutine and routine work processes?
The work of a research and development unit or organization is more difficult to describe than the process of making a cookie or a cooking pot. New-product development involves deliberations about what customers really want, what products will meet those needs, and what features the products can have that are within the core technology (most organizations need to stay focused on what they do well). Some of the answers to these questions are creative rather than linear. Identifying the core deliberations is more difficult in nonroutine work. The key questions often are: "What are we fundamentally about?" "What is our work?" "What are the core deliberations?" In FCFP, the same types of meetings are held for both work processes, but in nonroutine work processes, getting clear about the answers to these key questions pervades all of the redesign process.

Are there benefits to organizations that go through the FCFP work design process in addition to the redesign?

American culture has been characterized as outcome- and event-driven. To the degree that this is true (and in our experience, outcomes are totally absorbing to many leaders), important *process* outcomes will be overlooked. FCFP builds into an organization a capacity that it did not have before. The process of coming together in system-wide groups, sitting around tables, and doing work effectively together across departmental lines creates in the organization a new competence for work that most organizations do not have today. Smart organizations understand what has occurred and continue to do work this way in order to maintain this new capacity. Others, not recognizing what they have gained, continue in old patterns and the competency atrophies.

Anyone who has seen the energy and ideas that get released when people who are not used to being involved begin to see the whole process and think about and understand what they are part of will understand that this new way of working can be translated into ways of working on all kinds of systems issues, not just redesign.

Chapter Nine

Real Time Work Design

It is "zero-minus-one" day to launch in Clinton, Illinois. In the back of a very large conference center ballroom filled with seventy-five white, cloth-covered round tables, two groups are forming. They are getting ready for a two-day Real Time Work Design (RTWD) event for Corning's Revere Ware Plant.

This is the first event in a series of large group meetings, whose purpose is to redesign the plant to create both a more competitive product and a better work environment. Because the plant changed ownership several times in the 1980s, worker-management relationships have had their share of uncertainty. In the current process, Corning hopes to create a sound basis for participation and collaboration. Across the room, I (Barbara) see Kathleen Dannemiller in the center of a group of people from the plant. They are the steering committee for the event, and they have been preparing for several months. Tomorrow morning, the whole plant, from the plant manager to the shop-floor workers, union and management, will walk in the doors 550 strong to spend two days together assessing their situation and beginning a work redesign process for the plant. Right now, they are immersed in last-minute issues and checks on what will happen tomorrow. As I walk by, I overhear Kathie saying, "Who are the customers who are speaking?" and I hear that there is some uncertainty about whether the customers who were invited are coming. Later, I hear Kathie Dannemiller checking to be sure that the lunch is set up so that no one will have to wait, because the design only allows thirty minutes for lunch.

The other group, and the one that I join, is the logistics staff for the event. This is our "staging day"; twenty of us, many of us consultants from all over the country, have flown in to lend a hand and at the same time learn firsthand how one of these really big events works. As I look out over this triple-sized ballroom, I try to imagine how more than five hundred people can work together. I know that our logistics team will make that possible, but I find it easier to imagine all the things that could malfunction than how we will provide a smooth process that allows work to occur.

We are managed by a logistics "czar"; she calls us to order and lines out the work for the day. We each have a certain number of tables as our territory. We are part of the Just-in-Time delivery system that provides materials to each table exactly when the consultants managing from the platform request them. For example, we deliver instruction sheets at the cue, "Please pick up your copy of the directions for the discussion task and post your answers to the questions on a flip chart." Some of us will handle microphones during the report and general discussion periods. Others will "sweep" the corridors to get participants back into the ballroom as breaks end. Everyone will be responsive to requests from the platform for any help they need. We are expected to be in the ballroom at all times and to be alert to the environment, for example, to the temperature as well as the participants' needs. We will feel good if we can perform like a well-run drill team! Our goal is for the logistics to happen so flawlessly that the participants are unaware of them.

Once we are clear about our role, we spend the rest of the day preparing materials—in particular, what seem like hundreds of boxes for a very complex simulation of an airplane factory, "Viper," that will be run on the first day. At 8:30 P.M., as I drag myself off to bed, I realize that we have each spent almost twelve hours working very intensely preparing for tomorrow's launch. I am very excited and my back aches.

Day One

When I arrive at the breakfast area near the ballroom at 7:00 A.M., I am surprised to see that a few participants are already there. I cannot quite imagine almost six hundred people spending two days with each other in this big space. As they arrive, they get a name tag with a number on it and instructions to find the table with the same number on it. We already know that these are max-mix tables, planned by the steering committee to include a diagonal slice of the organization at each table, mixed by gender, skills, function and any other dimension that seems important. The chances are that they will not know many of the people at their table.

The room gradually fills up and the level of conversation increases. People wander across to see people they know; inspect the red, white, and blue packets that are at every place; investigate the hotel; and make side comments about how they decided whether they were going to come or not. I notice interest, joking around, some discomfort, and waiting.

At 8:00 A.M., the two consultants, Kathie Dannemiller and Paul Tolchinsky, are on the platform with the head of the union, the plant manager, and the plant manager's boss. The short kickoff includes a talk on why we are here and what we need to do in the next two days from the perspective of each person on the platform. The consultants explain the schedule and how the group will work together, and by 8:30 everyone is into the first activity, "Telling Our Stories." The eight people at a table each take three minutes to introduce themselves to the others at their table. They do this by reflecting on four topics that are on the table:

1. Who I am and where I work

2. Changes I've seen since Corning bought us (good and bad)

3. How confident I feel that we have the right people to lead us successfully into the future

4. What I need to get out of these two days to feel that it is worthwhile.

The tables are self-managing. This means that they are instructed in how to rotate the roles of facilitator, timekeeper, and recorder. After everyone has been heard, the group is told to discuss the common themes they have heard and write them on flip charts. Seventy-five recorders go to the sides of the room, where they pick up one of the flip charts stacked against the wall and sail it across the sea of tables until each table has one. The recorders write the significant similarities and differences as well as what people want from the two-day event. Then they call out a sampling of what they have written so that everyone gets a feel for what was said in just a few minutes. Among the "call-outs" are loud and sometimes testy voices raised for more pay, better machines, more security. All of the input is cheerfully accepted and acknowledged by Kathie or Paul.

Next the participants are invited to take part in the Viper simulation, which represents a production organization that builds planes. Half of the people in the ballroom move down the hall to another large space and, during a coffee break, the logistics team reconfigures the ballroom into eight production lines. In the first round, each thirty-person group builds planes in a hierarchical and functionally organized structure that cannot be changed. At the end of the round, the lines calculate how many planes they built that the customer accepted and how much they spent to build them, and they produce a profit-and-loss statement. The results are less than exciting. Few groups get more than one or two acceptable planes out the door and costs are very high. Before the second round, they discuss the experience. They feel constrained by the rules and organizational structures and do not feel very successful. Sarcastic comments like "This is too much like work" are heard.

After a box lunch that appears on cue and is in everyone's hands almost simultaneously, the next task is to redesign and run an organization that can build a plane that customers will like better, that can be produced more efficiently with better quality, and that creates working conditions that the employees are happy with. The results of the new work organizations are much better. Customers are happier and accept more planes. As we look at eight profit-and-loss statements posted on the stage, we see that most organizations are making some profit. Is it clear that what has happened in the simulation is a metaphor for what needs to happen at Revere Ware? Some people seem to get it; others are still in a "wait and see" mode.

It is hard to believe that it is already mid-afternoon. The time has raced by and everyone has seemed to be engaged as well as having some fun.

Now it is time to hear from Revere Ware's customers, in this case, the stores that feature their product. Once again, we are all together in one ballroom. The customers are very candid. (I know that they have been asked not to pull any punches but to be very straightforward in their comments.) As the customers talk about what they like about dealing with Revere Ware and the product and what creates problems for them in their business, they have everyone's total attention. The tables are intensely engaged as the participants discuss what they have heard and develop questions that they want to ask the customers. Tables are called on randomly and their questions are direct. There is a very frank and thoughtful discussion of both Revere Ware and of its competition. When the discussion is over, everyone in the room has a clearer understanding of what the customers need, what they like, and what is creating problems for them.

It is the end of the first day. Everyone fills out an evaluation of the day and leaves. The steering committee sits around reading the evaluations. They have planned a dinner work session to read and summarize the evaluations and make any necessary changes in the next day's program. Most of the evaluations are noncommittal, not very positive, not very negative. Kathie Dannemiller is unsurprised and reminds the committee that she had predicted that the first day's evaluations would be toward the negative. It is a pattern to be expected, especially given the troubled history of this plant.

Day Two

The next morning, everyone is back in force. It is to be a day to remember, a day full of emotional volatility, a day of very hard and very good work. It begins with a summary of yesterday's evaluations, the steering committee's response to them, and today's plan. In the first activity, each table is assigned to be one of Revere Ware's three biggest competitors. The tables are given material about that competitor and everyone listens to three role plays in which the competitors talk about their strengths and what they think about Revere Ware. Then each table is asked to identify with the competitor and plan a strategy that will "sink" Revere Ware. After that, each group asks, "What must we at Revere Ware do differently if we are to beat them? How do we reduce the risks?" Energy is high for this activity. Flip charts fill up with suggestions for change and improvement.

The flip chart suggestions for each competitor are posted together on separate walls. People gather around to read them and to express their own views of which ones are most important by "voting" with five colored adhesive dots that they place on their strategic choices. The three competitor role players summarize the voting results and announce them after a coffee break.

Next a labor-management panel from a United Air Lines facility that has just been through a complete redesign process comes to the platform and tells the story of how they worked together to try to become more competitive. They are candid and challenging. They identify with how people at Revere Ware are feeling. Again, the tables discuss what was said and shoot back questions to the panelists. I can sense the mixed feelings in the room. Some people find the idea of meeting the challenges they are confronting very energizing, whereas others are skeptical.

After an early lunch, the participants are reassigned to tables in the functional groups in which they work. The plant and company leaders come to the platform to talk directly about what they want and hope to do and what they need from everyone in the plant. The tables again discuss what they have heard and are recognized to ask questions and make statements. This is the most emotional session. All the negative history in the plant that has created mistrust pours out. Doubts are expressed about whether the plant will be sold again and whether the management will have enough continuity to make any investment pay off. At the same time that anger and frustration are being expressed, others are developing a more hopeful attitude. They are feeling ready to move and to try again. The consultants believe that where this kind of affect exists, it must be ventilated before people are able to move on. The secret is not to get stuck in it.

The next piece of work is to look a year into the future and describe what could be happening then that would make us proud and happy. This begins the process of creating a vision for the plant. All the table reports are posted and again, with a set of colored sticky dots in hand, everyone roams around and votes on their top choices. Then the leadership reports on the top vote getters.

Finally, in functional groups, each table is assigned one of the key production processes and asked to think about what could be done differently to make it go better. This work is posted and shared. This is also the preparation work for four subsequent one-day conferences that are to be held in the following month to work at redesign and improvement in more depth.

At the end of the day the leadership talks about the next steps and what has been accomplished in these two days. Then the group evaluates the second day (much more positively) and goes home.

Next Steps

During the next two months, a series of four smaller conferences, each consisting of representatives from the whole plant, examines in more detail the external market and the technical and "people" issues in the plant. They then agree on revisions in structure and process to create a more effective work process and a better relationship between management and the work force. During this same time period, a new union contract is ratified.

Six months later, much better union-management relations are in place, new products are coming onto the market, some restructuring of management for better alignment has occurred, and quality is improving. On the downside, no improvement has been made in cycle time (due in part to not including one core process in the redesign) and an important customer was lost, which has had an impact on the bottom line. It is probably too early to judge the pay-off of this work. Unfortunately, the American mentality of looking for short-term results often interferes with achieving the longer-term results of this type of intervention by changing the conditions before the results are in. We hope that Revere Ware will have the opportunity to complete this system change and examine the results before that happens.

Real Time Work Design

When Paul Tolchinsky became a partner in the Dannemiller group in 1994, he had been an active STS practitioner for a number of years. This expertise, combined with Kathleen Dannemiller's large-scale strategic design skills in dealing with the whole system (described in Chapter Five), allowed Kathie and Paul to develop a new large-scale process, called Real Time Work Design (RTWD), for doing organizational redesign much faster than with traditional STS methods.

In RTWD, a research and design team is created as the guiding mechanism for each project. This team includes representation from management and the union and all levels of the workforce. Ideally, it has from eight to twelve members. Because they carry heavy responsibilities, working from five to ten days between events, their normal job load may be reduced during the project. They work closely with the external consultants and typically report to a senior manager or sponsor of the redesign. The first task of the team is to get educated about redesign methods and to clarify with their sponsor the parameters of the redesign. Will the whole system be redesigned or just certain processes? What, if anything, is taboo? What of the old must be kept and honored?

The flow of events in RTWD is represented in Figure 9.1. In this method, the process is anchored by two whole-system, two- or three-day conferences that involve everyone in the organization that is to be redesigned. In the vignette above, we described the first, or launch, conference, in which the whole plant was in the room. Everyone was invited to attend and almost everyone came. The other conference that involves the whole system is the implementation conference. For obvious reasons, when it is time to implement a redesign, the more who participate, the more who will understand, contribute, and support the process.

The Launch Conference

The launch conference has three purposes. First, it educates everyone about the current business environment and the challenges facing the company. It answers the "why" question of redesign. Second, it educates experientially about what redesign potentially can do and gives people a real-time first cut at looking at their own work process. Third, it gives employees the opportunity to interact with management over their concerns about both the company and the proposed redesign process. It gets everyone "reading off the same page."

Role of the Research and Design Team

After each conference, the research and design team assesses the outcomes of the previous conference and plans for the next conference. It also does whatever specific research and analysis are necessary as input to the next conference. In this case, the team learns to do a technical analysis of the work flow and creates three or four process models of what the production process might look like if it were free of problems, waste, and redundancies. The idea is to push people's paradigms about what a truly efficient process would look like. Based on this work, the team defines the purpose, outcomes, membership, and agenda for the process conference. Finally, it checks out its design for the next conference with a group that is a microcosm of the whole organization.

The Process Conference

The process conference is a two-day event that gives a critical mass of the stakeholders in the production or service process the

Figure 9.1. Real Time Work Design.

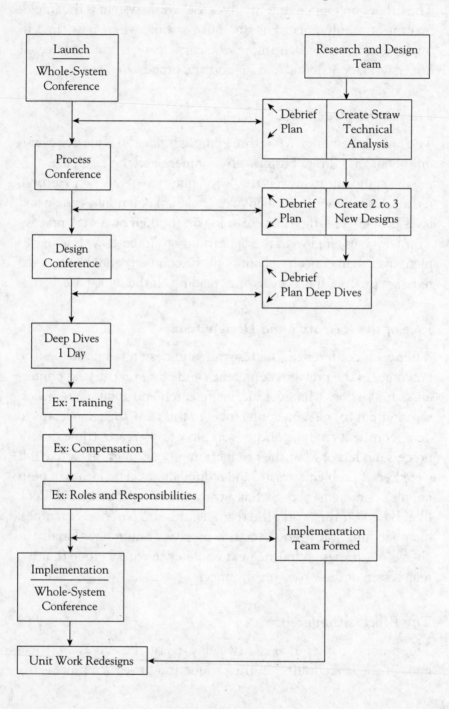

opportunity to think carefully about how work is done and to understand what their current state is. Then, they interact with the research and design team's process models. Finally, they have the opportunity to reconfigure the work process in any way that makes sense and that improves the process. Notice that this is more than is done in traditional STS redesign, where variances are identified and targeted for change but the basic work flow remains the same. The product of this conference is a redesigned, and often reengineered, process model. This conference involves subject matter experts in all the major stages of the work flow, cross-functional representatives, and as many levels of the targeted work unit as possible.

Interim Activity: Research and Design Team

During the process conference, videotapes are made of the major activities and edited down to an essential fifteen minutes for use in feedback meetings with members of the system who are not attending the conference. These meetings are full of information and interaction. They are held both at the work site and in general meeting spaces.

At the same time, the team works to flesh out the details of the process model developed at the process conference. Once this is completed, they can prepare several possible new organizational designs to stimulate thinking at the design conference. Topics include work unit boundaries, mission and purpose statements, and a sampling of the core, support, and administrative tasks of the possible work groups. Like the process models, these are intended to create possibilities and discussion among the conference participants. Again we see the interesting point and counterpoint that occurs between the research and design team and the conference process. Notice that the team is creating divergent possibilities and breaking the mind-set. When the research and design team creates divergent possibilities, the conferences can become more convergent and agree on solutions.

The Design Conference

The next two-day conference involves cross-functional representatives and a max-mix of employees at all levels who will be affected by the new design. During this conference, participants agree on a set of principles to guide their final decisions and work together to build their own organizational models using the provocative designs suggested by the research and design team. The end result of these two days is agreement on an organizational model that is the consensus of those who are present.

Interim Activity: Research and Design Team

The research and design team must decide which support process will be most critically affected by the new design. They select the processes that are the focus of the one-day deep-dive conferences. This team also communicates with people who were not at the design conference about what occurred there, using the video feedback meeting format described earlier.

The "Deep Dives"

This is a series of one-day conferences focused on critical system support issues. They help in anticipating and solving a problem that has plagued traditional work redesign: if an organization waits until the new work design is finished before beginning to redesign the critical system support processes that are needed to make it successful—for example, compensation and training—it has waited until it is too late. The discrepancy between the new design and the old support system processes is likely to sabotage the new design. The Deep Dives focus attention on these processes. Customers and suppliers get together and talk about what is needed from the supplier—for example, human resources—if the new system is to work. This allows support functions that create pay systems or worker education to begin early in planning to bring their function into alignment with and support of the new design.

The Transition from the Research and Design Team to the Implementation Team

At implementation, the work of the research and design team is finished. An implementation team is formed to oversee the implementation process and provide periodic checkpoints along the way.

The Implementation Conference

Finally, the whole system comes together to hear about all the work that has been done and to participate in planning the implementation of the redesign. This eventually leads to mini-conferences in work units as they participatively do their own implementation. These vary from half-day meetings to meetings that take several days. Individual-unit implementation is guided by principles that are very congruent with the principles in the Emerys' Participative Design method (discussed in Chapter Ten)—for example, creation of whole tasks and control by those who do the work.

How long does it take? If you are familiar with the process of traditional STS redesign, which often takes several years, you will be delighted to think about being able to move from launch to implementation in something between three and six months. The time for the implementation process is harder to predict, because it happens in smaller work units and can occur quite quickly or be spread out a bit over time. The pace of implementation is affected by continual monitoring of the process; what happens in the business environment, often including the larger corporation; the signals coming from upper management about the urgency of the change; and the maturity of the affected groups.

RTWD, like the Conference Model® and Fast Cycle Full Participation, is grounded in STS theory but involves far more members of the organization in the redesign. It has the capacity, as we saw in the vignette that began this chapter, to literally involve the whole system in the redesign process in one place at the same time.

Chapter Ten

Participative Design

It is Tuesday, 8:30 P.M., in a small town in the northern part of the state. You are the vice president of a manufacturing company and plan to meet Wednesday with one of your company's divisions, located just outside the town limits. You have just arrived, and since it is the middle of the second shift, you decide to stop in at the facility to see how things are going. At the main office, you have heard people talking about how, for several years, this division has used an entirely new approach to redesigning work, called Participative Design. You are not sure how it works, but the division has greatly reduced its costs, and people have assured you that things are working very well indeed.

As you enter the continuous process manufacturing facility, you are surprised by the fact that you do not see anyone around, either workers or supervisors. Finally, you hear some noise in a back room and wander to the rear of the facility. As you enter the room, you see seven people clustered around a flip chart, sketching out the flow of the processes and discussing them with great animation. They do not notice you, so you listen in on the conversation and realize that some of the people are from Maintenance, some from Administration, and some from Operations. None of them is a supervisor. You are amazed at how well they are working together, how much they seem to respect each other's views and opinions, and how intent they are on solving the problem.

Participative Design, a method of involving work groups in redesigning their own work, is unique because it starts at the bottom of the organization and works its way up. Created by Fred and Merrelyn Emery in 1971, Participative Design was developed in response to difficulties the Emerys encountered in implementing traditional Socio-Technical Systems design (Emery and Emery, 1989).

As the Emerys noted, the social structure controls an organization's productivity and is the source of workers' responsibility for and investment in organizational change (Emery, 1993). However, a shortcoming the Emerys noted is that the STS design group often becomes an elite entity controlling the process. Cut off from the majority of the workforce, the design group can engender resistance or apathy because it usually (1) deals with only a small, "specialized" part of the system rather than the system as a whole, (2) never changes the underlying bureaucratic structure, and (3) draws little or no ownership from the majority of workers.

Participative Design evolved from this knowledge about design groups as well as from the Emerys' deep commitment to workplace democracy. Traditional organizational structures follow a bureaucratic structure, whereby the first-level line supervisors control the work of subordinates. However, with Participative Design, the workers themselves control their own work. This "workplace democracy," as the Emerys use the term, is not about having workers vote for the new president of the company or decide on new marketing policies. Instead, it is about having people design, manage, control, and coordinate their own work. In Participative Design, the central assumptions of STS (acknowledging that the core social system actually manages the technical system, not the other way around) are affirmed while circumventing the drawbacks traditionally encountered with "isolated" design groups.

One of the Emerys' special contributions is Participative Design's bottom-up approach, which is unlike any of the other work redesigns in Part Three. In Participative Design, the people who do the work are responsible for controlling and coordinating it; the work is *not* controlled by the level above.

Six Critical Human Requirements

In addition to these democratic principles that guide Participative Design, it has six clearly defined "critical human requirements" that are the criteria for meaningful and productive work (Cabana, 1995a, 1995b). As workers redesign their work, they test their ideas against these criteria. The requirements are:

1. *Adequate elbow room:* People need to feel that they are their own bosses and that their actions and decisions (except in exceptional circumstances) are not being constantly scrutinized by a supervisor.

2. *The opportunity to learn on the job and keep learning:* People can learn only when they both are able to set reasonable yet challenging goals for themselves and are able to get feedback on results in time to make corrections, rather than being called on the carpet after the fact.

3. *Variety:* People need to be able to vary their work, thus avoiding fatigue and boredom. In addition, variety allows people to set up their own satisfying rhythm of work through which they can be most productive.

4. *Mutual support and respect:* Instead of being pitted against each other in a "someone has to win and someone has to lose" scenario, workers need to give and receive support and respect, enabling the group to truly cooperate and use all members' skills to the fullest.

5. *A sense that one's work meaningfully contributes to the social welfare:* This sense of meaningfulness includes the quality of the product or service and its worth to the community as well as the worker's knowledge about and understanding of the product or service's end use or purpose.

6. *A desirable future:* Workers need a career path that allows them to continue or increase personal growth as well as to increase their knowledge and skills.

As Steve Cabana notes, "Meeting the needs of these six require-ments means restructuring the workplace. This naturally happens when responsibility for interpersonal coordination and the *control over effort and the quality of work is [sic] located with the people who are actually doing the work*" (Cabana, 1995b) [emphasis ours]. We have also learned that several of the people who do other redesign work often use these six principles during implementation.

When employees learn these design principles, they acquire ways to analyze and redesign work. In addition, learning these prin-ciples means that workers also possess a very good tool for interact-ing with management. Bob Rehm, a consultant on Participative Design conferences, has told us that when he returns to groups a year or so after they implement Participative Design, everyone is still discussing what they and management are doing and how it does or does not fit the democratic design principles. He says, "The ongoing dialogue is very powerful and keeps everyone on their toes" (Rehm, 1996).

The Skills Matrix

A key element used in Participative Design is the skills matrix. After people analyze and get feedback on their skills, they can establish learning goals for themselves. Traditional organizations usually have one worker for one task, with workers perceived as replaceable parts. With the skills matrix, several workers control one function. In self-managed groups, this is called multiskill devel-opment. Everyone knows several jobs and can help out and take care of the work if someone is on vacation or ill. Multiskilling also greatly increases the human interactions around the task, because people understand the other task as well as the challenges and dilemmas that surround it.

The Process

Figure 10.1 illustrates the process flow of Participative Design, which is implemented through a Participative Design workshop, explained in more detail below. The Participative Design workshop begins with an organization-wide educational process. This is important because, for most organizations, the result of Participative Design is a fundamentally different organization, not just in structure but also in culture and values.

The *educational workshops* begin with senior management. Even though Participative Design's focus is that the workers who are doing the work will control the work, it is essential for management to be on board with the Participative Design concepts. Educational workshops help managers to understand the difference between bureaucratic structure and its outcome and participative structures and their outcomes. After working with the management, facilitators conduct educational forums throughout the organization to educate all workers at all levels. It is important to note that a gap in time may occur between holding the educational forums and undertaking the actual redesign. For many organizations, this is an important period because it gives them a chance to reflect on and absorb the new participative paradigm.

In the next step, senior management comes up with minimum critical specifications against which all designs that are developed must be measured. An example of a minimum critical specification would be "No increase in staff" or "Less than a 5 percent increase in budget" or "Maintain the same level of customer service." In

Figure 10.1. The Participative Design Process.

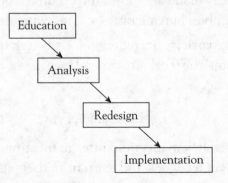

determining these specifications, management must be extremely careful to find a balance, providing enough specifications to give participants some guidance but not releasing an avalanche of "rules" that will smother the creative process. During a Participative Design workshop, these minimum specifications are posted so that the parameters are clearly visible to everyone.

After the minimum critical specifications are in place, each work unit holds a Participative Design workshop that follows these steps:

Analysis Phase

1. Top management opens the redesign workshop and briefly shares the organizational purpose and the minimum critical specifications. Then they depart.

2. Work unit participants analyze how the job is currently done and assess how much this falls short of meeting the six critical human requirements.

3. Participants assess all skills required to do the work of the organization under redesign and determine who has each skill. This helps to provide information for possible multiskilling and is useful in later training needs assessment during the implementation phase.

Design Phase

4. Work unit participants draw the existing work flow and organizational structure so that everyone knows where decisions are currently made and how far the current organizational chart resembles bureaucratic or democratic design principles.

5. Work unit participants redesign for a better, more natural way of doing the work, incorporating the six critical human requirements.

Implementation Phase

6. Work unit participants hold interim meetings with other groups to get feedback and learn from their efforts.

7. Work unit participants develop measurable goals and targets.

8. Work unit participants spell out training requirements and coordination needs (external and internal).

9. Work unit participants test the work, again, against the six principles.

10. Work unit participants finalize the design.

11. Management returns to the workshops to listen, discuss, and negotiate with the group.

In each workshop, most participants would be from that work unit, although in some cases, representatives from the management hierarchy could be present. If, for example, supervisors were invited, they would be available to listen and provide feedback, if asked, but otherwise they would not attempt to run the meeting or direct its outcome.

In Participative Design, unlike other work designs, external stakeholders are not physically present. Instead, data are collected from external stakeholders ahead of time or, in some instances, stakeholders can be brought in to give input and to answer questions. They are not, however, part of creating redesign. This is significant and is based on the Emerys' belief that the people building the design should be the ones who are, in the end, responsible for implementation because they are the ones who have to live with it and make it work.

An interesting technique sometimes used in the Participative Design workshop is *mirroring*. According to Rehm (1996), in mirroring, two groups (for example, Marketing and Production) work on redesigning one group, then the other. On the first day, both groups would work to redesign Marketing; on the second day, both groups would redesign Production. The advantage of mirroring is that it can provide an outside design, perhaps even an out-of-the-box one, that might be creative and effective.

After each work unit at the bottom of the organization completes its redesign, the next phase in the process is to have their supervisors attend workshops and develop their own redesign. Each group should, of course, have full knowledge of the designs that came out of the first group's meetings. They are not, however, required to follow that group's lead. Participation in these meetings generally does not exceed thirty-five to forty people.

Next, the design process—with each level having met and produced its own work design—flows up through the various organizational levels. Often a series of parallel Participative Design workshops is used to allow every person to participate. We imagine that, as this process moves along, participants consciously or unconsciously integrate features of other designs into their own. Even so, the total number of designs is often very large. At this point, therefore, participants hold a "town meeting" in which the designs are discussed and integrated as much as possible. Finally, one design is selected by the workers.

Let us say, for example, that workers in a particular company produce three designs: A, B, and C. Most of the workforce preferred design A, but the senior management preferred design C. It is crucial to the Participative Design process for senior management to go along with the workers and choose design A, because the workers will be enthusiastic about and willing to support their own plan. If management forces design C on the workers, the result will be tremendous resistance from the very people needed to implement the design. Of course, whatever design is selected, it must meet the minimum critical specifications established at the beginning of the process.

Case Studies

A number of companies have successfully used Participative Design. Syncrude, a consortium of oil companies that remove tar from sand and then convert the tar into petroleum products, has successfully used this process. The company brought together over one thousand managers, supervisors, assistant supervisors, and technical experts in a three-phase approach. First, in the exploration or learning phase,

Syncrude used Search Conferences as planning sessions over a day and a half to "unfreeze" the old ways of doing business and to introduce the substantive changes that self-managing structures could bring about.

In the second, or implementation, phase, each department used Search Conferences to identify the desirable futures for that department. The only constraints were that the functions had to fit corporate strategic goals such as budget, production quality, and workforce numbers. These conferences were followed by Participative Design workshops, in which workers created designs for their work. Then all designs were reviewed and one was chosen. A key question, focusing on the "most desirable future," was used to help participants to effectively sort the many design options that had been generated.

The final phase—adoption of procedures, policies, and practices—is still moving forward. However, since initiating the Participative Design effort, Syncrude's cost per barrel has dropped by roughly three to four dollars and is the lowest in the industry, and production has increased from sixty million to seventy-nine million barrels per year with the same equipment.

Another example of how Participative Design has been used comes from the work of Bob Rehm with the U.S. court system. New management in the Los Angeles bankruptcy court office wanted to modernize and restructure the workplace to increase productivity and teamwork. This office processes all the legal documents of the court, manages the court docket, and provides services to the judges, lawyers, and court customers. The Los Angeles division consisted of about one hundred staff members, both workers and managers. They were organized along functional lines, with different units providing docketing, filing, magistrate services, and intake. Each function had a typical bureaucratic structure, with each level of management responsible for the work of the next level down.

The Participative Design process of analysis, redesign, and implementation planning took five working days for the entire court. On Monday morning, fifty people, a cross-section of the whole organization, arrived for the first workshop. It was held right at the workplace: no expensive off-site location was needed. The clerk welcomed people, restated the purpose and management's commitment, and clarified the minimum critical specifications for the design process. People seemed surprised when the clerk introduced the Participative Design workshop managers, who were clerks and deputy clerks from other parts of the country. They had all been trained in Participative Design and were experienced in using it; they were present to support the groups as they worked on the tasks. The participants immediately knew that management meant business.

Once the clerk left, people got right down to work analyzing their human needs and the extent to which they were satisfied with the organization as it currently functioned. The group consisted primarily of black and Hispanic women, with a minority of whites and men. No supervisors were present, but they were on call in case anyone had a question. From the beginning, energy and noise levels were high, as people enjoyed talking freely and openly about their work environment.

People broke into small work groups to brainstorm new designs. It quickly became clear across the groups that some people wanted to move to a more cross-functional organization. They ended up calling the cross-functional teams case management teams, with each judge having his or her own team. The work goal of each team would be to deliver a complete array of services to its judge, including docketing, filing, magistrate services, and intake. To begin with, each team would need workers from each functional area. Over time, however, the teams would manage their own multiskilling to make sure that they had backup for every function. They also decided that they could immediately handle their own work and vacation scheduling, participate in performance evaluations, and rotate some team leadership jobs.

The participants finished by identifying some important implementation issues emerging from the design, such as a participative way to pick new teams. At noon on Tuesday, they completed their workshop and left in a spirit of enthusiasm and self-confidence, yet wondering whether management would really go along with the plan.

On Tuesday afternoon, fifty more people, another cross-section, arrived for the second workshop. The people from the first workshop decided not to spill the beans to the second group because they did not want to influence their work. Nevertheless, there was a lot of buzzing during breaks. The second workshop was a repeat of the first, step for step. By the end of Wednesday, the group came up with a design that was strikingly similar to the first group's. The team boundaries were quite similar; only details differed.

On Thursday morning, participants who had been selected by their peers met to compare notes and converge their designs, if possible. Their charge was to combine designs, but not to do any new design work. The group did its combining and presented both a final design and implementation ideas to the whole organization, including management, that afternoon. Considerable discussion, questioning, and some arguments took place. By the end of the day, people gave the design a thumbs-up.

Before the workshops had begun, the clerk had arranged for the court's facilities management department to be ready to make changes to the office setup that weekend. At the end of the meeting, the clerk asked for volunteers to meet immediately to begin planning for the new office design, which would happen that weekend. On Friday, the managers and supervisors had their own Participative Design workshop to design their own work in light of the new organizational structure. Upper management discussed their new roles relating to strategy and boundary management. The supervisors also took themselves out of the hierarchy, re-forming themselves as a technical service group. At the close of business on Friday, management reported their own design work back to the rest of the organization. Implementation started Monday and continues to develop and evolve.

To date, U.S. court organizations that have used Participative Design include Seattle, Washington; Sacramento, Los Angeles, and San Francisco, California; Atlanta, Georgia; southern Florida;

Austin, Dallas, and San Antonio, Texas; Chicago, Illinois; North Dakota; Nevada; and Utah. Although the specific design varies in each court system, in all systems, 100 percent of the workers in the court organizations participated.

Reflections on Participative Design

Participative Design addresses a major concern about many of these approaches: as exciting and meaningful as change "events" are, if they do not alter the underlying structure of the organization, does lasting change occur? What Participative Design tries to do is to extend the culture of participation and responsibility that is created in a Search Conference to the entire organization. In the final analysis, Participative Design acts as leverage for creating systemic change by locating responsibility at the level where the work is done. To do this, organizational structures must be designed that are democratic and nonbureaucratic.

Unfortunately, what happens in many cases is that new participative designs are adopted and laid right over the existing bureaucratic structure, resulting in what is called a "mixed mode." The new method may indeed be superior and ultimately more productive, but if the bureaucratic structure is not changed, the old and powerfully entrenched structure will co-opt the new system, and no real change will happen in spite of the good intentions and optimism of all the participants.

The Emerys say that when autonomous work groups do not work in this country it is because most work redesign happens, essentially, in a mixed mode; management always has the prerogative to pull rank and shift the process back to the old bureaucratic, nondemocratic methods, even when that management is ostensibly invested in a new way of doing things (Cabana, 1995b). For this reason, we are aware that Participative Design may not work in many of our corporate climates. If it is attempted in climates that are not truly committed to changing the structure, the only noticeable result will be increased cynicism among workers. If they go to workshops and come out enthusiastic, then see all their work either co-opted or ignored, they will become hardened against any process that promises change.

However, we hope that management will think about these participative designs and give them a chance, realizing that it will take commitment to keep the system moving forward to new levels of participation and to keep it from sliding back to the status quo. At Syncrude, for example, employees at all levels are working on creating an entirely new governance structure that has more employee participation and is designed to continue the process even during a change in leadership. Thus, for example, a new CEO cannot come in and dismantle all the work that has been accomplished.

Part Three Summary

As we have seen, the Conference Model®, Fast Cycle Full Participation Work Design, Real Time Work Design, and Participative Design are all methods that allow people to redesign the work process for both their own and the company's benefit.

The major similarity between the methods is that they all rest on the Socio-Technical Systems framework created by the work of Fred Emery and Eric Trist in the 1950s. As we noted elsewhere, this work was slow in being adopted in the United States. When Trist moved to the United States and began to consult to places like General Foods in Topeka, Kansas, with Jack Sherwood and Don King of Purdue University and Dick Walton of Harvard University, his ideas influenced not only those who consulted with him, but those they trained. For example, Bill Pasmore and Paul Tolchinsky got their degrees at Purdue with Sherwood and King.

STS practice only began to really flourish in the United States during the 1980s. By then there were training centers at several universities. More than a few internal organization development practitioners learned STS when it was introduced in their company and eventually went out on their own as external consultants. Most of the practitioners mentioned in this part were practicing traditional STS redesign at about the same time that large group intervention practice was emerging. The fundamental STS concern about understanding the environment and creating a best fit between the technical process and the social system process is embedded in these combined large group and STS methods. Large groups add the ability to allow many more people to participate; they have more influence on the design and their ideas and knowledge are used in the design process. Large group methods also shorten the time frame and keep information about the redesign process available to everyone.

We have chosen not to include a comparison chart at the end of this part for several reasons. First, the Conference Model®, Fast Cycle Full Participation Work Design, and Real Time Work Design have so much in common that we believe the differences to be minor. All three differ from Participative Design, as we have already indicated in Chapter Ten. We note that difference below. Second, the three STS methods are continuously being experimented with and improved upon. Client needs cause innovations. The practitioners talk to each other and are influenced by each other.

Having acknowledged the strong similarities, we will compare these methods on a few dimensions. One interesting difference between these methods is how much of the whole system is in the room. Because versions of the Search Conference and Future Search are used at the beginning of the Conference Model® and Fast Cycle Full Participation and are limited to groups of 35 to 100, designs using these methods tend to use representative groups and to be smaller than RTWD. However, a great deal of experimentation is going on and we would not be surprised to see this hurdle overcome in the near future.

The more interesting question is "When do you need everybody in the organization to be involved in an event and when will a critical mass of stakeholders do?" Dannemiller and Tolchinsky have a preferred answer: you need everybody at the beginning and at the end. Others are quite flexible. One client of the Pasmore group wanted the whole system to participate in the design and ran a series of three design conferences that allowed everyone in the plant to be involved. There, the outcomes of each conference were integrated into the next conference. The answer seems to be that this decision is worked out with the client, given the constraints of time, money, the ease of getting everyone together, the values of the client, and the pace at which the change must occur to meet the client's demands.

Another important difference has to do with participative democracy and what it means to the originators of the method. To Merrelyn Emery, as we understand it, it means that people should be able to control and be responsible for the work that they do. In her framework, therefore, work is designed using correct principles from the bottom of the organization up. Others in this part admire and use the Participative Design method when they have set the boundaries of the work unit and are engaged in implementation. They believe that the preferred way to work is to establish a participative process for involving the whole system first in a total process redesign that sets an overall framework. This takes seriously the managers' rights as well as the workers' and allows everyone to participate equally. It also allows for a parallel process to deal with the infrastructure changes that are needed.

This is a complex debate with real theoretical differences that we should not ignore. On the other hand, we need to point out that the overarching theme in all these methods is the active participation and empowerment of the whole workforce in being responsible for and proactive about the work setting. For many organizations, this represents a sea change in worker attitudes and behavior from the present bureaucratic culture where workers compete with each other or are passive in the face of authority. And, as we have pointed out in many places in this book, it represents an equally major change for much of management.

Because of their clarity about the value and belief system underlying Participative Design, the Emerys are also clear about the fundamental shift in values and culture that using their methods will require in many organizations. For this reason, they often begin work with a system through education. At Syncrude, for example, they spent most of the first year in the system running workshops that helped people to understand these principles and the level of change that might be expected. All of the work design practitioners in this part are very aware of the need for education in the system before work design begins, and they all include system education as a first step.

It is natural to look for evidence of differences in effectiveness between the methods. Unfortunately, not enough research has been done in comparing the different approaches to make any definitive statements. It is also true that in big system-design projects, so many factors are at play that comparing interventions is a task for only the most intrepid. In other words, we do not know if one method is better than another. All of them have their success stories, so in some situations, they all work.

Part Four

The Methods
Whole-System Participative Work

One of the fundamental problems in bureaucratic, hierarchical organizations is the lack of open communication between units about issues and problems that the organization is experiencing in getting its core work done effectively. More often, there is blaming and finger pointing between departments but not much effective action.

Four methods can be used as large group interventions to bring the system together to do real work in real time on problems, issues, and agendas that need to be addressed. One of them, Large Scale Interactive Events, is not presented as a chapter because it was described in detail as Real Time Strategic Change in Chapter Five. This method can be adapted to all kinds of problem-solving and cross-functional coordination issues.

Two of the methods in this section, Simu-Real and Work-Out (see Part Four Figure), are approaches that bring people together to address current issues in the workplace. Simu-Real promotes organizational learning at the same time that it explores issues. Work-Out is a direct attack on problems the organization is experiencing, with all the relevant stakeholders in the room.

The third approach, Open Space Technology, is a unique method for getting organizational issues that people care about on the table for discussion and, if the time is right, for action. The issues it deals with can be current problems or a discussion of future decisions and options.

Part Four Figure. Comparison: Large Group Methods for Whole-System Participative Work.

SIMU-REAL
Purpose: Real-Time Work on Current Issues, Test Future Designs, Learn About System
Donald and Alan Klein

- Organization Selects Issue for Work
- Room Arrangement Reflects Organization's Structure
- People Act Their Organizational Role
- Periods of Stop Action and Reflection
- Decision Process Agreed to in Advance
- 1 Day
- 50 to 150 People
- Facilitator Needs Expertise in Process Consultation

LARGE SCALE INTERACTIVE EVENTS
Purpose: Problem Solving
Dannemiller and Jacobs

Uses Same Methodology as Real Time Strategic Change. See Description, Part One

- Many Different Uses

WORK-OUT (GENERAL ELECTRIC)
Purpose: Problem Identification and Process Improvement

- Improvement Target Selected
- Employee Cross-Functional Meeting
- Process: Discuss and Recommend
- Senior Management Responds Immediately
- Champions and Sponsors Follow Through to Implementation
- Follow-Up as Needed
- 1 to 2 Days

OPEN SPACE TECHNOLOGY
Purpose: Discussion and Exploration of System Issues
Harrison Owen

- Least Structured of Large Group Technologies
- Divergent Process
- Large Group Creates Agenda Topics
- Interest Groups Form Around Topics
- Periodic Town Meetings for Sharing Information Across Interest Groups
- One Facilitator Lays Out Format, Ground Rules, "Holds the Space"
- Requires an Understanding of Large Group Dynamics
- 1 to 3 Days

Chapter Eleven

Simu-Real

It is a warm July day and the fifty administrative and professional staff members of a rapidly growing community mental health center are arriving at a local high school for a one-day activity known as Simu-Real. They have been told that the day will be spent exploring issues that are troubling the center—growing tensions between older and newer organization members, professionals, and the administration—and generating ideas for improvement.

As participants enter the gymnasium, where they will spend the day, they quickly notice that their organization is laid out on the gym floor: the three satellite offices sit in three corners of the room, and the administration and central office programs are placed near the center. Groups such as volunteers, graduate student interns, the substance abuse program, and research and evaluation are all assigned a space that maps their relationship to the center (see Figure 11.1). As people register, they are asked to join their own groups, which range from two to ten people, in the assigned space. Signs labeling each area, as well as chairs, desks, and other props, are in place, provided by the planning group.

The director opens the event by restating the purpose as well as his concern that participants need to explore and make decisions about issues that have resulted, in part, from the very rapid growth experienced over the past few years. The director also indicates that he is willing to be responsive to advice and agreements reached by the group as a whole during the day. He then introduces the consultant, Don Klein, who has worked with the planning committee over

Figure 11.1. Simu-Real Layout.

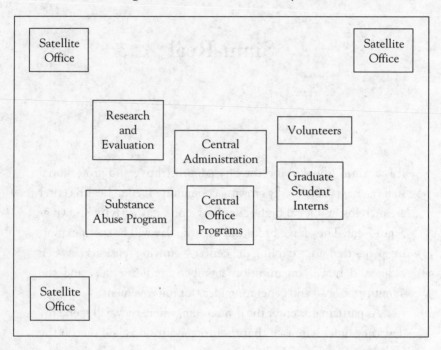

a three-month preparation period, during which the event was designed.

Klein comes forward and talks about the intergroup stresses that participants have revealed in interviews with the planning committee and about how the issue to be addressed in this workshop was formulated from those data. Next, he describes the pattern of work. There will be three one-hour periods of interaction. Participants are free to talk with anyone on the floor, to propose action in relation to any other group, and to try out new activities. They will do this as real organization members with all of their real roles and responsibilities.

After each one-hour period of total group "simulation," a thirty-minute "stop-action" period will be held for reflection about what everyone has observed. The consultant as well as the participants will contribute to this analysis. After each period of reflection, the participants will go back to work on the issue. After the third cycle, in mid-afternoon, a designated group of decision makers, including the center's director and representative administrators and professional staff, will meet in a circle, in front of everyone present, and make decisions based on what they have seen and experienced. Before the final adjournment, everyone will have an opportunity to express his or her thoughts about the events of the day.

With this introduction, the day rolls forward and the first interaction period begins. Noticeable in the first hour is a sense of uneasiness in some groups, a hesitancy to act across group lines. As the day progresses, however, the pace gradually picks up and participants become more animated. They begin to interact more freely; some even look like they are having fun. Groups form, discussing various issues of concern and garnering support for their ideas from other groups. By mid-afternoon, a growing consensus has formed about the need for some restructuring of the agency and the need to provide the opportunity for more input into decision-making processes. What is especially remarkable is the sense of the whole organization that everyone now has. In particular, there is increased appreciation of the satellite offices' points of view.

In the decision-making session, the first steps are taken toward a modified matrix structure that will be fully confirmed and running in two months. A cabinet system that allows rotating representation from three operating areas and four centers is proposed and agreed to, with the proviso that it will be reviewed in one year to see if it is creating the desired sense of participation.

A feeling of optimism and goodwill is evident as people begin to leave the session, making comments such as "I can't believe we got so much done," "There really is hope," and "We're going to hold 'em to it!"

The Development of Simu-Real

Simu-Real was created in the mid 1970s by Donald Klein (1992), a professor at the Union Institute of Cincinnati, Ohio, and an organizational consultant with a long history of interest in community development. In his work with organizations, Klein was struck by two dilemmas those organizations faced. One was how difficult it was for many organization members to know about and appreciate the roles of people in other parts of the organization. Because people cannot see the whole organization, they tend to view the organization solely through their own experience, which can create real difficulties in intraorganizational decision making. The second dilemma was the complexity-beyond-grasp dilemma. That is, so many things are going on in an organization at any one time that no one can take it all in. Because of this, people tend to assume that they cannot change anything either.

Klein (1992) built on his previous simulation work in community meetings to create Simu-Real, a structured simulation of a real situation to give an organization a clear look at how it works on tasks and issues. Simu-Real can help people in organizations to:

- Grasp the whole system in its complexity
- Create a way to see the simultaneous transactions that go on in the organization
- Determine what needs to be changed

Organizations tend to follow the old, internalized ways of working unless they become aware of the internalized system, analyze how it affects them, and determine how to change it. Because members of most organizations do not really understand the functions, responsibilities, needs, and wants of people in other areas of the organization, they tend to get caught up in their own issues and lose sight of the whole. Simu-Real is a marvelous vehicle for creating new perspectives and allowing organization members to participate in understanding and fixing problems that affect their work life. We will now describe the processes in more detail.

Getting the System in the Room

When an organization sets up a Simu-Real event, the first step is to use a very large room and to set it up to reflect the organization's actual structure—its physical plan. Each functional department is represented and staffed by its own members. If an organization has branch offices, they are represented by tables on the periphery of the room and staffed by their members. Headquarters are set up in the middle of the room. In addition, the room setup reflects any informal systems that exist, such as the group of people who meet around the water cooler to discuss events and ideas, or the informal lunch group where important issues are thought to be discussed. The idea is to replicate the structure of the organization accurately so that when the group begins to address a problem, the organizational structure of the Simu-Real room faithfully reflects the real functional structure of the organization.

Addressing the Task

The Simu-Real design focuses on one systemic issue or problem that has implications for everyone who attends. This issue is decided in advance by a planning committee, whose task is also to make sure that all functional components are physically represented in the meeting room. By focusing on a single, predetermined task and, as Klein (1992, p. 570) notes, "by eliminating the need to observe the usual social amenities, engage in shop talk, and carry on informal conversations about unrelated topics," participants can crystallize weeks' or even months' worth of real-time activity into a day-long meeting. Some participants have estimated that a one-day Simu-Real session covered work that would have taken a year to eighteen months to accomplish through the usual organizational channels.

Although complex systems problems are typically selected as issues, it is also possible to choose a more future-oriented agenda. For example, Simu-Real has been used to try out new organizational processes and structures.

Stop Action, Reflection, and Analysis

The process begins with the consultant having the participants work on the issue, for one hour, in any way they choose. As they work at their assigned task, the consultant observes what happens and how it happens. The participants also find their work periods to be extremely revealing about how they function in the organization and how the organization functions around them. After an hour, the consultant stops the action. Participants must stop what they are doing and spend the next thirty minutes thinking about what they have just done. The consultant asks, "What do you see?" "What does this mean?" or some other series of reflective questions.

Following this question and reflection period, the participants and consultant work together to analyze or diagnose the way the organization functions. They may analyze how they see their organizational structure working, how they perform certain tasks, or what assumptions they make about tasks and about each other. The consultant will also share his or her observations about what has gone on in the session. After the stop-action period, the participants go back to work. What happens between the reflection and the resumption of the task is Simu-Real's goal—a change in the dynamic of how an organization approaches or solves a particular task.

The Decision-Making Process

After what are usually three periods of stop action, reflection, and analysis, the end of the afternoon is reserved for decision making. Participants have agreed, in advance, that either a recommendation or a real-time decision, based on their observations, actions, reflections, and analyses, will come out of the Simu-Real design.

As Klein (1992, p. 572) notes, questions that can be explored at the planning stage include the following:

- Are decisions taken during Simu-Real advisory or binding?
- How are decisions ordinarily made in the organization?
- Should the organization use Simu-Real to explore a different approach to decision making?

- Should decision making be delegated to executives or to a representative subgroup of the organization?
- Is it preferable to give all participants in the Simu-Real event an equal opportunity to influence and participate in the decision making?

When the planning committee has answered these questions, it will find it easy to select one of the three forms of decision making that Klein (1992, pp. 573–574) suggests can be used:

1. *Executive decision making:* In the decision-making period, the executives discuss the decisions raised by the work of the day, using a fishbowl format with an empty chair that allows participants to join the circle temporarily to express their views. The executives have a real meeting and make real decisions for later consultation with, for example, the board or other stakeholders.

2. *Ad hoc decision making:* In this form, a representative group from the organization is selected in advance and known to everyone. They occupy space at a decision makers' table during the day as well as carrying their real organizational roles. At lunch they meet privately with the consultant to begin the discussion of what the decision issues are and how they will structure the public meeting. That meeting, which is held in mid-afternoon, is run as a fishbowl with an empty seat, as in the executive decision-making process. Naturally, this form would only be used for issues in which management is willing to abide by the decisions of a representative group.

3. *The decision-making table:* This form creates an experimental situation for decision making and raises issues of informal influence. A decision table with about twelve chairs is part of the floor plan and is labeled as the decision table. Participants are told that at any time when all the seats are occupied and the group comes to a consensus on any decision, it is binding for the organization. This means that others need to be aware

of what is going on in that part of the room. It also means that opportunities to influence are open to all. This decision process can be binding or it can be advisory (but simulated as binding).

Simu-Real in Action

A paper company in Georgia used Simu-Real to take a look at all the interfaces that self-managing manufacturing teams at the paper plant had to negotiate to conduct business, for example, with utilities, purchasing, finance, and suppliers of raw materials. They discovered and explored new ways to communicate and agreed on new ways of working together.

In addition, this company was going through restructuring, and the central manufacturing division was being transferred into another division. A corporate human resources representative came to the session to work out the transfer. Interestingly enough, she was never invited into the discussion. After the manufacturing teams had discussed their issues, the consultant turned to the human resources representative, who had been standing in the doorway, and asked her why she was there. She expressed her mission and said that she had felt completely excluded from the process. The rest of the group responded, suddenly realizing that their treatment of her reflected the dynamics of the manufacturing division's feelings about the transfer.

Using Simu-Real in the Future

Simu-Real is most frequently used as a method of examining, analyzing, and changing existing models of organizational structure and behavior. Another way to use it is as a way to test a proposed new business process or structure before launching it. For example, Eastman Kodak Company has discussed using Simu-Real to test a new budgeting process before launching it, so that they can "debug" the process before it is fully implemented. This is similar to the portion of the Conference Model® (see Chapter Seven) in which the "patient" from Mercy Healthcare was taken through the system to see how much time a real patient had to spend at each part of the admission process.

Another extension of this method, which would emphasize its learning dimension more than that of decision making, might be videotaping the event for playback to participants at the end of the day. Participants enjoy watching themselves and also obtain significant insight about how they and their organizations function when they see it live on camera. Since Simu-Real is only beginning to be known, we believe that many ways to use it have as yet been unexplored.

Many of the methods described in this book have serendipitous learning effects on participants that they take back with them into the workplace. Simu-Real, more than other methods, has organizational and individual learning as an explicit goal. Although the process is active, the intended self-reflection results are more than the decisions that have been made. The whole organization will have learned about itself and this understanding will, in turn, influence the actions of individuals.

Chapter Twelve

Work-Out

Last year, while eating lunch at a restaurant in Connecticut, we overheard a woman at the next table say, "Next week I'm off to India to help with a Work-Out in one of our plants." This was the first time we had heard that General Electric Company's Work-Out method, which has proved very successful in the United States, was being used by General Electric's overseas operations.

The Work-Out process was created by Jack Welch, the CEO of General Electric, as a result of his frustration with the slow rate of change in many GE divisions and plants. His plan developed as a result of his experiences in the company's Crotonville, New York, management training center (Tichy and Sherman, 1993). Every two weeks, Welch would fly to the center to share his vision of GE with employees who were attending training sessions. During these highly interactive meetings, Welch challenged employees with his vision. He wanted people to operate in flexible, cross-functional work teams that would meet frequently to fix work-flow problems. He wanted to take the unnecessary work out of work.

The employees' responses to Welch's challenge were not exactly what he expected. Engineers, managers, and supervisors—new hires as well as established employees—vented their frustrations, complaining that the company bureaucracy prevented any real change from occurring. Underlying this frustration was the fact that GE had experienced many layoffs in its attempts to "delayer" the company structure. As a result, people had left, but the work had not. And, in spite of the layoffs, the structure had never really changed. Thus, workers had even more work and were still hampered by outmoded policies, procedures, structures, and duplicated efforts. Welch found that he was leaving the meetings feeling as frustrated as the workers he had talked with.

Kathleen Dannemiller (Dannemiller and Jacobs, 1992) talks about arthritic organizations in which work is hampered as it flows horizontally through stiff departmental joints. Vertical or hierarchical structures are often arthritic as well. In GE's case, contracts often required as many as *ten* departmental approvals. In addition, as one supervisor noted, he could authorize spending twenty-five thousand dollars to replace a valve but needed three levels of approval to purchase one hundred dollars' worth of office supplies. He and other employees attending training sessions at Crotonville told Welch, "We like your ideas, but we don't have the power to make these things happen." "Yell at your leaders!" Welch would retort. "I empower you!" Not surprisingly, not much changed.

One day, as Welch was returning to his office after attending a session at Crotonville, he and Jim Bowman, then head of the Crotonville center, cooked up the idea of "Work-Outs" to be run at major GE plants and divisions. The first Work-Outs were run as town hall meetings. Conducted off-site, they involved a cross-level and cross-functional group of employees from a division, led by teams of external and internal consultants. These were large group events of one hundred to two hundred employees, depending on the size of the division.

At first, the consultants did not address productivity, waste, or quality problems because they knew that employees would perceive focusing on a specific issue merely as preparation for another round of layoffs. Instead, during the Work-Out, groups of employees were asked simply to generate any issues that they thought were dumb, were a waste of time, or needed to be changed. Newsprint was posted around the room, and employees were free to write "the dumb things we're doing that waste time." They were then given dinosaur stickers to prioritize the "dumbs."

The terms "rattlers" and "pythons" were developed to describe some of the issues that surfaced. Rattlers were issues that made a lot of noise but were easily fixed. Pythons, on the other hand, made little noise but could quickly choke a process; they were much harder to detect and deal with. One example of a python occurred several years ago in GE's lighting division. Serious quality problems were occurring with a certain type of globe. Customers would receive their orders only to discover that many globes were in pieces. In a Work-Out session, teams were established to find the python. They carefully traced and examined all parts of the process, from manufacturing on down, eventually sending a team to actually ride on the van that delivered the globes to the customers. And they discovered that the problem lay, not in the quality of the globes, but in the packaging that was used for shipment.

An important rule for the Work-Out sessions was that no blaming and no complaining was allowed. If a worker did not like something, it was up to that worker (or work team) to develop a recommendation and an action plan. As these action plans were developed, each team picked a volunteer who would be willing, if the go-ahead decision was made, to make the change happen. This volunteer champion was often supported by a team of volunteers.

At the start of the Work-Out programs, Welch attended the meetings. During the work-team discussions of problems and the offering of action plans, the upper-level management responsible for making the decisions to implement these plans would leave the room, returning only at the end of the meeting to receive the team's recommendations. Rumor has it that if the workers' recommendations were reasonable and the upper-level manager procrastinated or balked, Welch would bang his fist on the table and say, "Sounds good to me. Let's do it!" Whether this story is true or not, what is true is that Welch's presence brought strong support for the process and sent a clear message to the decision makers.

In one of the divisions, prior to a Work-Out, the consultants had encouraged the vice president to guarantee that no one would lose employment as a result of the Work-Out and its recommendations. People might change jobs, but no job loss would take place. The implication was that this would free people to look closely at what positions were essential and where unnecessary levels existed.

This division contained three supervisory levels: regional managers, area managers, and section managers. At the start of the meeting, the vice president announced the employment "guarantee." As the meeting progressed, the area managers sitting together at a table had a heated discussion about whether they should surface what they had concluded—that their positions were unnecessary and could easily be eliminated. They asked, "Can we trust what the vice president said?" After much debate, they finally decided to trust the statement and presented their recommendation to eliminate their positions. The happy ending to the story was that the vice president was telling the truth. The structure was reorganized to eliminate the redundant management level, but the employees did not lose their jobs. Instead, they were transferred to positions where they could perform work that was actually meaningful to the organization.

Steve Kerr, the current director of Crotonville, reports some changes since Work-Out was initiated (S. Kerr, personal communication, 1996). There is substantially more legitimacy about raising issues of waste or quality or work-flow problems; therefore, Work-Outs no longer require Welch's presence. GE has also trained numerous internal facilitators, so external ones are no longer needed. Nor do Work-Outs need to be situated in off-site facilities. In fact, many plants have set aside space where cross-level and cross-functional teams can meet and discuss process improvements. Finally, meetings today will often include suppliers and customers.

Kerr states that the process has become so internalized that when workers get stuck, they will say, "Let's have a Work-Out and get this thing resolved." He also notes that because the process is now optional, some divisions or plants occasionally choose not to use it. Kerr feels, however, that because of Work-Out's success, most divisions and plants use it regularly.

This success has not been limited to the GE plants and divisions. The company has also trained many of its suppliers and customers in this methodology. As a customer, GE gets better service and more satisfaction because the Work-Out gets the bugs out of the supplier's system.

Here is a generic model of steps used in a Work-Out:

1. Choose a troubled work process for discussion.

2. Select an appropriate cross-functional, cross-level group and convene a Work-Out meeting.

3. Generate recommendations from work teams to improve work flow and eliminate unnecessary work.

4. Ask for a volunteer or teams who will take any recommendations that are accepted and see them through the implementation process.

5. Meet with the management, who must respond to the recommendations immediately. Latitude is allowed for negotiation and further study.

6. Conduct additional meetings as needed to follow up on the recommendations.

Questions About Work-Out

Have Work-Outs been used in unionized plants?
Work-Outs have been used successfully in both union and nonunion settings. One consultant told us that when a Kentucky company's large appliance division conducted a Work-Out, the union workers were cynical at the start of the meeting. They sat at the back of the room, listening to what they thought would be some new management "trick." However, during the Work-Out, a major customer came and talked to the group. The employees were galvanized by descriptions of the quality problems from the customer's viewpoint and were then more willing to cooperate with the Work-Out.

What have been some of the overall business results of the Work-Out process at GE?

Here are some examples:

- Savings of hundreds of thousands of dollars at some divisions
- Making to order instead of making to inventory
- Reduction in the time needed for a testing process from three to seven days to less than twenty-four hours
- Reduction in cycle time (in one instance, from fifty-nine days to seven days)

Further Elaborations on the Work-Out Method

Many of the consultants who facilitated the original Work-Outs have gone on to elaborate and refine the Work-Out methodology and are currently applying these methods to other organizations. For example, at present, a major blue-chip, high-tech company is using a version of Work-Out to address a core business issue: reducing its cycle time from order entry to customer, which was twice as long as the competitors' cycle time, using the following steps:

1. The sponsor, a manager responsible for the core business process, presents the critical business issue needing attention.

2. A planning group is established to examine the issue, define the questions, and decide who should be involved in a three- to four-day meeting to help correct the problem. These meetings usually range from 40 to 120 people, depending on the issue.

3. Recommendations are presented to the sponsor. We are told that at least 85 percent of recommendations are accepted. Recommendations use the following original GE format:

    The issue
    The symptoms

The root causes

A cost-benefit analysis

Recommended actions

This format also includes "Who?" "What?" "When?" and "Resources Required" lists. Planned follow-up meetings occur at thirty, sixty, and ninety (full implementation) days.

The Effects of Work-Out

Organizations have often allowed structures, policies, and procedures to get in the way of workers' ability to succeed at their work. We think that Work-Out gives workers an opportunity to surface the problems that otherwise might get swept under the company rug, and then to make appropriate changes.

Work-Out has also proved to be a powerful process without the need for major structural changes. It attacks the often-ridiculous policies and procedures that interfere with getting work done, or, as one consultant put it, "It reaches the low-hanging fruit." Perhaps the greatest contribution, however, is the cultural changes that have resulted from Work-Out:

- It improves union relationships.
- It involves people who have never been involved before in the problem-solving process.
- It speeds up decision making.
- It makes senior management more accessible to employees.
- It changes senior management's perception, helping them to recognize that the people who do the work are the ones who know how to improve it.
- It helps employees to recognize some of the complex decisions faced by senior management, particularly in the area of cost benefits.

- It allows people to challenge why work is done the way it is.
- It develops new cross-level and cross-functional working relationships.
- It improves both lateral and vertical communication.

Chapter Thirteen

Open Space Technology

Three hundred twenty principals of a worldwide consulting group assembled in the conference center ballroom on the morning of the second day of their annual meeting to begin three days of Open Space on the successful future of their organization.

I (Barbara) could tell that this was clearly not business as usual. The meeting on the preceding day had been typical of other annual meetings: strategic information and encouragement from top management, awards for outstanding consulting engagements, updates about internal processes, and service line meetings occurred in a predictable flow.

Day One

But now it was Tuesday morning, and instead of more speakers on a preselected theme, the consulting organization was trying something very new. This was immediately evident when everyone walked into the room. Instead of lecture-type seating, 320 chairs were arranged in three concentric circles, with a large open space in the middle. Nothing else was in the room except for a few hand-printed signs on newsprint around the room that said things like "The Law of Two Feet" and "Whoever Comes Is the Right People!" Many paused at the door as they arrived, looking around with raised eyebrows and trying to decide where to sit. The Open Space event was kicked off by a short talk by the general manager about positioning the organization for the future. During his talk, he made several comments about how unusual it was for the organization to try this kind of meeting. Although he was obviously not comfortable trying to talk to people in a circle, his message about the future was clear and upbeat.

He then introduced Harrison Owen, the creator of Open Space, who comfortably picked up the theme and described in a few minutes what they would be doing and how they would do it. He told them that they would create their own agenda and run their own meetings for the next two days around issues that they really cared about. He described the importance of a few simple principles and laws for the working of Open Space and suggested that they use the Law of Two Feet to guide their behavior and only be in places where they felt they were learning and contributing. (We will explain the Law of Two Feet and the principles later in the chapter.) He then talked about the Four Principles:

1. Whoever comes is the right people.

2. Whatever happens is the only thing that could have.

3. Whenever it starts is the right time.

4. When it is over, it is over.

If you were used to traditional conferences, he said, you might not appreciate the bumblebee and butterfly roles that often develop in Open Space. Some people flit from group to group, cross-pollinating the conference (bumblebees); others are beautiful butterflies and never quite get to any meetings, but others find them and often new ideas emerge. Side murmurs and appreciative laughter were heard as he spoke. Not only was this different, but they were being given permission to do whatever seemed right for them. Who had ever come to a national meeting like this before? Was this for real?

It soon became obvious that this was indeed what was going to happen. Harrison invited all the participants who had a passion about an issue and who were willing to be responsible for it to come to the center of the circle, write their issue on a piece of newsprint, sign their name, and come to the microphone and announce their topic and their name to the group. Then they were instructed to go to the wall labeled "Community Bulletin Board," select one of the Post-it Notes that gave a location and time for a meeting, paste it on their topic sign, and hang it on the wall under the day they had selected.

There was a pause when everyone was probably wondering, as I was, what would happen if no one came forward? But Harrison just looked interestedly at people and "held the space," allowing the process to develop. After a bit, someone got up, picked up a piece of paper, and began to write on it, then another, and another, until a dozen or so were writing and then going to Harrison's microphone to announce their topic and their name. When the initial flow waned, people who had been hesitating were urged to take the plunge and a number did. In about fifteen minutes, more than fifty topics were announced and posted.

After being given a final opportunity to propose a topic, the participants were asked to go to the wall and sign up by writing their name on any and all topics that they wanted to attend. Harrison suggested that in the interests of public safety, with over three hundred people, they should not all go at once. So people sat around and chatted until there was space. In another fifteen minutes most of the topics had some names on them; a number were of high interest and attracted many signatures.

The Post-it Notes were arranged so that each controlled a $1\frac{1}{2}$-hour time slot at a particular meeting place in the conference center. Eight time slots and 15 meeting spaces were available in the two days after the first morning, creating 120 meeting spaces. Once a person declared a topic and picked a time and place, her or his responsibility was to show up and convene the meeting. After the meeting was over, this person was to type up a summary of who was there and what happened on one of the fifteen computers arranged around the other walls of the ballroom. Harrison was there to help with any problems, but the program was simple and self-instructing.

As a low-profile visitor, I wandered in and out of five or six meetings during the first day and more on the second. I noticed that even though most rooms had classroom-like fixed seating (not the optimal arrangement for Open Space), some members usually turned their chair around for an arrangement more conducive to discussion. Some groups were clearly led by the convener; others had free-flow give-and-take. One group of six or seven was in the midst of working out a complex technical problem. Another group of twenty was debating the necessity of certain corporate policies and appropriate actions to take. A third group was inventing new processes for integrating and educating midcareer hires. The groups were relatively stable, with occasional people joining or leaving. One group that didn't have time to decide on the action steps they wanted after a lively discussion noted that a similar topic was being discussed on the next day and agreed to show up in that time space. Later that day I happened to overhear a member of the group telling the convener for the next day that he was "being taken over" by today's agenda. He seemed interested and agreeable; of course, if he hadn't been, the group could have found other space in which to convene.

Open Space was the main agenda, but in the hall by the ballroom doors were sign-up sheets for two or three demonstrations of new software products available to the group. I had never been to an Open Space where other agendas were present. In this case, the time slots paralleled those of Open Space and the demonstrations appeared to be well attended without detracting from the main event. I also noticed smaller groups of people, in central gathering places, who were meeting and working intently, apparently on business issues. Because this was a group from many countries, and this was the one time during the year when they were all together, Open Space provided a lot of agenda flexibility and time and space for easy networking.

During the afternoon, reports began being filed, printed, and posted on a wall near the ballroom entrance. As people discovered them, the readers began to collect and converse. The page-length reports were numbered in order of their printing and posting so that, on subsequent visits to this "news room," it was easy to remember what we had read. "The Evening News," or final session of the first day, held in the ballroom at 5:45 p.m., was brief. A few announcements were made, along with a reminder about the next day's "Morning News" session. The evening was a "free night" and people went off to do whatever they had planned.

Day Two

The second day began as the first had ended, in the large circles in the ballroom. Harrison asked if people wished to raise any new topics. A long pause followed, and finally one man came out to write on the newsprint. Several people followed him and another eight to ten topics were posted. Harrison then explained that a book summarizing all the discussions would be published and in their hands the next morning. All they had to do was to be sure that if they convened a discussion, they had their summary report typed into the computer by 6:30 that evening.

The second day had a relaxed and mellow feeling. Groups were meeting all over the place, but the strangeness had worn off and this way of working was becoming familiar. People regularly checked in at the wall to see where they wanted to go or to read the now-long list of reports. At that evening's "Evening News," some announcements were made and Harrison explained what would happen the next day in order to prioritize the sixty-seven issues that had been reported out.

At 6:30 p.m., when the computers shut down, Harrison printed out 102 pages of reports with a table of contents, a one-page description of the event that produced the book, and a simple ballot for voting on the top ten priorities. This went off to the copy center, where it was reproduced and bound with a cover page overnight.

Day Three

At 8:30 the next morning, the delegates assembled to hear a much more structured schedule described. First, they were to pick up a copy of the book and read and select their ten most important issues; by 10:00 a.m., they were to have keyed in their votes on one of the computers. After a thirty-minute break, they were to return to the ballroom to hear the results. About 10:15, the frequency distribution was produced and Harrison made the call that there were fifteen top vote getters. The title of each of the fifteen top priorities was posted on a flip chart. The fifteen charts were distributed around the ballroom and adjoining anteroom space. People were instructed that for the next hour their job was to visit any or all of the stations and record two types of information on them: (1) any other related issues and (2) action steps that they wanted to see occur. Whoever convened the session was asked to record the comments of those who came by.

The final event of this Open Space was a commentary by the firm's manager about each issue, what had been written about it, and how it would be carried further. When I asked Harrison what else he might have done with more time, he said that often groups form around issues after they have been identified to work further and make proposals. The morning took the form of a convergent process that felt very familiar and much more like traditional problem solving. It has, I think, been added to Open Space in the interest of bringing some convergence out of the rich divergence that Open Space provides. When people have sampled all the dishes on the buffet and eaten enough, a natural momentum turns them to thinking about what comes next. In this setting, that means asking, "What are we going to do about all of this?" Prioritizing and moving toward action are reasonable next steps to focus what has occurred.

Finally, in this setting, unlike others, a one-page evaluation was handed out. Generally, Open Space is whatever it turns out to be, and no evaluation occurs other than what happens as a result of the event. In this case, the organization insisted on some kind of data collection. In fact, people were already doing this informally. I heard people say that this was a great format for networking.

When I talked with the internal organization development manager who sponsored the event, she reported that after the event people were generally very favorable in their comments. Open Space allowed for a whole-system discussion of issues that were on people's minds; at the same time, it met the networking needs of a global organization that only meets occasionally.

What Is Open Space?

The history of Open Space Technology is an often-told and still engaging story. The originator, Harrison Owen (1992), made a major time commitment a few years ago to planning and orchestrating a conference on organizational transformation. After the conference was over, he realized that despite hours of detailed planning and implementation, some of the best moments had occurred during the coffee breaks; he wondered if it would be possible to create a conference that was "all coffee breaks" (Owen, 1992, p. 3).

As he thought about this, he found himself reflecting on his experiences working in Africa, especially on the form of the African village as a place where communication flows effortlessly: villages are arranged in a circle with a central marketplace or gathering place and have a community bulletin board. Using these ideas, he created the simple design described in the vignette you have just read. Here are the elements in conceptual rather than story form.

Organizing for Open Space

The first hour of Open Space organizes the meeting for the full time (one, two, or three days). People assemble in a room that has enough chairs for all participants, arranged in a circle. If the meeting has many participants, say five hundred, the circle may be three rows deep. The room is empty except for the circle of chairs, with a pile of cut pieces of newsprint and many markers on the floor or a table in the middle. The facilitator of the Open Space—only one person no matter what the size—stands in the middle of the circle, usually with a cordless microphone.

The Purpose of the Meeting

First, the facilitator speaks with the group about the reasons they are gathered, the theme of the meeting, what it is hoped they will talk about and do. Although this talk may only be five to ten minutes long, it is critical because it sets the tone and engages participation. In order to do this effectively, the facilitator needs to spend time in the organization and work with a planning group as well as prepare personally.

Rules and Norms

Next, the facilitator talks briefly about what Open Space is and the rules or norms for operating in it. The emphasis is on telling a few stories about how other groups have successfully organized and managed themselves using this technology in the past, and on raising the expectation that an exciting and useful process will take place within this group. This is also the moment when the facilitator asks the group to start thinking about what they really care about vis-à-vis the theme and mentions that, in a little while, they will be asked to let others know what they really feel strongly about and what they are willing to be responsible for as an issue.

Having planted the core concepts of passion and responsibility, the facilitator goes on to describe the processes that make Open Space work. The first rule is the Law of Two Feet, which encourages people to engage their energy where they want to. This means walking away from any discussion where they don't feel engaged or where they are not learning or contributing, and finding something that is important to them. This first law usually gets everyone's attention. The idea of only being where you are learning and contributing sounds slightly heretical, maybe even impolite, but at the same time delightful and tantalizing. For the very responsible and overly rule-oriented, freedom not to attend sessions or to float from one to another is created in the roles of "butterfly" and "bumblebee." Bumblebees flit from group to group, cross-pollinating the conference. They say things like "I was just down the hall and that group is talking about the same issue that just came up here, but they were saying . . ." Butterflies may never get to a session but can be seen in the lobby, in the bar, or at the pool. Often they attract others who feel the need for a "time-out" from the intensity of the discussions. Sometimes, in these groups, creative new ideas develop that then flow back into the conference.

In addition to the "Law of Two Feet" poster on one wall, the Four Principles are posted and described in the introduction. They also help to create norms and attitudes toward the Open Space process. "Whoever comes is the right people" means that the quality of interaction is what counts, not how many come or who they are. "Whatever happens is the only thing that could have" means that rather than having rigid expectations, participants should be prepared to be surprised and to be open to the moment. "Whenever it starts is the right time" urges people to pay attention to the spirit of the event and to let go of the natural bureaucratic type of thinking that tries to slot and control creativity and movement. "When it is over, it is over" is a principle that usually gets a pleasured murmur of assent. How many of us have sat on and on in meetings where the agenda was finished and the spirit had long since departed, but where we did not feel free to leave? In Open Space, everyone is encouraged to take the time that is needed and let go when there is no more to say.

These laws and principles are wonderfully liberating. They make people smile and take a different attitude toward the meeting and their participation in it. The laws and principles are also apt to produce a bit of anxiety. Whoever heard of getting three hundred people together for three days with no preplanned agenda? This newness and anxiety, if it is not too intense, also provides a motivation for movement.

Creating the Agenda

The main event of this opening period is setting the agenda. People are asked to consider what they feel passionately about in regard to the meeting theme. If they have a real concern and are willing to take responsibility for showing up at a particular time and place and initiating a discussion about their topic (and typing notes about the session into a computer after it is over), they are asked to come into the center of the circle, write their topic on a piece of newsprint and sign it, and then come to the microphone and announce their name and topic to everyone. The next thirty minutes or so is taken up with this process. Sometimes, there is an initial rush to the center, at other times a pause before the flow begins. Owen (1992) reports that groups of twenty-five to fifty usually produce at least thirty issues; in groups of one to two hundred about seventy-five issues will surface.

After people have announced their topic and name, they go to a wall labeled "Community Bulletin Board," which is divided into sections corresponding to the number of days of the Open Space and the time slots (usually $1^1/_2$-hour blocks) available for discussion. They select a time and place by pulling a Post-it Note with a time and place off a separate chart, sticking it onto their discussion announcement, and posting it in the space reserved for their day and time on the bulletin board. In a very short time, the wall is covered with topics, organized in time blocks and with place designations clearly stated. From that moment on, the bulletin board becomes a central meeting place for the conference, the place participants go to find out where things are going on.

Sometimes the participants notice that two topics are similar and suggest combining them. The general rule is to leave them alone unless the conveners really feel they want to combine the issues. Having more groups results in a richer discussion. Sometimes conveners will switch times so that people interested in related issues can attend both sessions.

Signing Up

Then, the participants are invited to take a pencil or pen, approach the wall, and sign up for any and all discussions that they are interested in attending—even two in the same time slot. As soon as everyone has signed up, it is time for the first session to begin. (As must be obvious by now, these events need to take place in hotels and conference centers with numerous small breakout areas, and preferably where the Open Space is the only event in the facility.)

From this point on, the conference pretty much runs itself, except for two periods at the beginning and end of each day, when the entire group gathers in a circle, called "The Morning News" and "The Evening News." These are thirty-minute community gatherings where people may speak about how the conference is going, propose new topics and post them, or say whatever else is on their mind or in their heart.

The News Room

The other gathering place for the conference is outside the news room (the computer room), where all reports of group discussions, who attended, and what was said are posted. This occurs in conferences of two or three days. A bank of computers is set up in a workroom and loaded with a simple word processing format for entering information about each discussion. Conveners come in and enter their summary, which is then printed out and posted.

The Role of the Facilitator

It may seem that the Open Space facilitator hasn't much to do after the opening session. In terms of the usual role of scheduling and controlling activities associated with "facilitation," this is certainly true. On the other hand, the facilitator's real role is to "hold the space": allowing the process to develop and intervening only if anyone is interfering with others' rights to choice by dominating or insisting that everyone must go along with his or her ideas. The facilitator also must understand systems and large group dynamics at a fairly sophisticated level. Several of the stories in Owen's book (1992) demonstrate how not taking action can be just as important an act in holding the space as doing something.

In other words, the technology is straightforward and it is possible to set up and structure an Open Space by reading Harrison Owen's book (1992). What happens in Open Space, however, is always new and unpredictable. Therefore, figuring out how to hold the space is not always either simple or easy. Owen and the regional networks provide a number of training programs around the country each year (see the Appendix for more information). In addition, an annual Open Space on Open Space is usually held the weekend before Thanksgiving, where Open Space practitioners gather for two days to discuss their work and issues of mutual interest.

Questions About Open Space

What kinds of agendas lend themselves to Open Space?
This is a hard question to answer, because many people use Open Space for a variety of purposes. Harrison Owen has collected some reports of events from people who were willing to write about them in his book *Tales from Open Space* (1995).

One type of Open Space brings people together who do not work regularly with each other around a specific purpose or theme. The National Education Association invited teachers, board members, and administrators to a conference on enhancing education in America. Lifelong learning as a core activity of business was the topic of a conference in India. Women's ways of leading and men's work in the men's movement were the topics of two conferences for women and men, respectively. The U.S. Forest Service assembled their own people and invited all kinds of stakeholders, from business to environmental groups, to a conference on access to public lands. These were all special events out of the routine of everyday organizational life.

A number of instances can also be found of using Open Space in the regular life of an organization, especially in the annual meetings of large organizations that are located around the world or around the United States. The worldwide consulting group described earlier used Open Space as part of its regular annual assembly. The Presbyterian Church U.S.A. held a three-day Open Space with five hundred representatives just prior to its official national meeting.

Organizations quite often select Open Space to help them create a vision or strategic mission for the organization. Accor hotel group of France found it so useful that when they merged with Wagon Lits they found that Open Space was helpful in putting the two cultures together. Rockport Shoes had a three-day Open Space for the whole company in order to reposition the company and create ideas for new products. Du Pont and Owens-Corning have also used Open Space for new-product development and to reposition a product category. Albany Ladder used it to open up nontraditional markets for a new product they had developed. A social welfare agency gathered to position their organization for new opportunities. A rural health center selected Open Space as a way to empower employees and change the nature of working relationships in the agency. In a similar vein, a large avionics defense plant that was making a transition from a traditional hierarchical organization to a team-based one found that Open Space helped people to experience the processes required of the new team organization by fostering initiative, responsibility, and cooperation. They found Open Space so useful that sixteen Open Space events were carried out throughout the organization's various departments.

What does Open Space really do?
Like other systems events, it gathers the whole organization or collection of interested parties in one place and enables them to talk about the topics as a whole. Therefore, communication changes dramatically, and people have a sense of the whole and a voice in the process of change. This can be especially useful in dispersed-network organizations where people do not get together regularly.

The thing that is really unique about Open Space, however, falls under the expression that is one of the ground rules of Open

Space: "Be prepared to be surprised." This intervention allows people to temporarily restructure the organization around interests or "attractors," people with similar energy, or issues. It makes visible the underlying energy patterns of the organization. When these interests connect, new ideas and outcomes are likely to emerge. As Janice Greene comments (Owen, 1995, p. 138), "What we tend to do in western society is fix the outcome then decide and complete the steps to reach it." In Open Space, people focus on interests. If outcomes emerge and catch people's interest, they may become reality, but the name of the game in Open Space is following your passion and not worrying about where it will lead.

How do you know when the right time for Open Space has arrived?
Harrison Owen says that there are three criteria. First, Open Space should be used for complex issues that involve a whole system. Second, Open Space works well in situations of conflict or divergent interests (although we assume that some situations may have such intense conflict that it would not be advisable). And, finally, it should be used in situations where it's impossible to think of anything else to do!

In our view, enough experience with Open Space has accumulated so that we can venture a few more ideas about when to use it and when not to. First, the nature of the issue is critical. When Rockport decided to hold their Open Space (Deutsch, 1994), they were at a critical point in the life of the company. They were just completing two very successful years, but the competition was moving in and they had few new products in the pipeline. It was a critical moment in the company's history. Rockport chose to share it with employees and engage them in a search for a new future, including new innovations in the product line. We think that this is an excellent example of the kind of moment that is ripe for Open Space. Very recently, Open Space practitioners across Canada have been organizing a series of meetings to discuss separatist issues among Canadians.

The consulting group described in the vignette above used

Open Space during their annual meeting. People came with expectations of participating in a standard type of annual meeting, even though they were told in advance about the event. The early part of the meeting met those expectations. We think that this does not make an easy transition into Open Space. Despite this, evaluations of the event were very positive. (Harrison Owen's advice to use Open Space last if you are going to combine it with other events is certainly correct.)

The right time and the right topic are clearly key. If the issues are too big or too vague or unclear, they will create lack of focus. If they are too narrow or defined, they will not provide enough room to be creative and they will not engage the imagination. Especially to be avoided are clients who have a narrow vision of specific outcomes that they want. They should not try Open Space.

This last comment takes us into a discussion of what leaders need to be and do to make Open Space successful. The most common problem cited among case writers about Open Space is the negative effect that leaders with autocratic and controlling styles have on these events. It is hoped that they will not be attracted to them. However, in fad-hungry America, some leaders are more interested in doing the "in" thing than in what makes sense for them. In Open Space, leaders need to be present and to participate the same way everyone else does. They set boundaries for the topic and the parameters for the work, but after this, they need to let go of control. If participants feel that they do not have full support to move on their own energy wherever it leads them but must second-guess what the boss is thinking, the process will not work. Consultants, therefore, need to work carefully with the executive group beforehand to ensure that they know what type of effect they can have on participation. In the consulting group example given in the vignette, top management agreed ahead of time to participate fully, but during the event, they were often seen doing business on phones and in the halls rather than being active in sessions. This affected the way others viewed and participated in the event.

Finally, expectations are key and affect what participants do and how they react. If people expect specific, countable outcomes, they may miss the significant gain in individual responsibility and initiative that occurs. If people expect to sit back and rest while they hear others make presentations, they may not like being challenged to declare their passion and take initiative. Each organization will need to think carefully about the expectations that people are likely to bring and how to position people for the event. This is not easy, because explaining Open Space often leaves people confused: "What do you mean, there's no agenda? How can you have a good meeting without an agenda?" Again, at this point, leadership needs to signal their faith and hope that everyone will give it a try and to explain enough about the event so that people feel reassured.

In all organizations, people become very anxious at times because of the high degree of uncertainty that is present. They are afraid for their jobs, afraid of changes in their alignments, or afraid of what may be required of them. Consultants and clients need to make a carefully considered judgment call about whether this is the right time for Open Space.

Open Space is also a very challenging experience for many people, especially those who have lived and moved in organizations that are characterized by tight supervision, command, and control. We have wondered if organizational cultures exist where Open Space simply would not work, where asking people to be proactive about their own interests is so orthogonal to the way their life is that they will find it impossible to respond. We leave our readers with this question to ponder. We suppose that such organizations are unlikely to select Open Space in any event.

What happens in organizations after the big event is over?
This critical question is asked about all the interventions in this book. In the case of Open Space, we have anecdotal evidence that in some settings Open Space sets off processes that do indeed continue.

Open Space as a technology developed out of the organizational transformation movement. Many people who believe in Open Space as practitioners also are committed to helping organizations become more participative and self-managing settings. Of interest here are not the specific, countable outcomes that may represent the work of an Open Space event, but the changes in the way the organization functions, the culture change that Open Space may produce.

The Center for Rural Health in Hazard, Kentucky, used Open Space to encourage a new norm in the organization. According to Kepferle and Main (1995, p. 41), "People who care passionately about a problem or opportunity have the *right* and the *responsibility* to do something about it." They only agree to observe the following constraints:

1. There should be widespread notification of meetings that are open to all.

2. Solutions and ideas must be communicated widely for discussion and input.

3. Solutions cannot hurt others.

4. Solutions should maximize limited resources.

5. All actions must be in line with the organization's central mission (Kepferle and Main, 1995, p. 41).

No constraints exist on who can call a meeting, what can be discussed, when to have meetings, who can attend, or what information is needed for the meeting to be effective.

In the large avionics defense plant mentioned earlier in this chapter, Open Space was used throughout the organization to make the transition to a team-based culture following downsizing. The method is credited with changing communication patterns in the organization in dramatic ways, bringing new people together and deepening old interactions. Leaders and supervisors learned to listen in a new way (Huntington, 1995).

In both these cases, management was openly and avowedly trying to create changes in the culture in a direction that is aligned with what Open Space asks participants to do. Open Space gave the organizations practice in precisely the behaviors management was asking for. No wonder transfer took place!

How long should an Open Space be?

Open Space can be one, two, or three days long. One day is long enough for a good discussion. The Public Broadcasting Service brought their whole corporate staff together for a discussion of the possibilities represented in a new satellite that moved them from 5 to 500 channels. In one day, they had a rather full exploration of the issues and of different views of how to proceed; they left knowing a great deal more about what others thought and what the options for development were.

In a two-day Open Space, it is possible to have a discussion and make a record of it that all the participants can take home with them. This is done using the computer setup described earlier. The second day also allows overnight "soak time" that may lead to the emergence of new issues and proposals during the "Morning News."

Three days of Open Space is the recommended maximum. It is reported that after this the process has spent itself (or maybe three days of talking nonstop is enough for anybody). The third day is an opportunity for reformulations and convergence to occur. Or, if the client organization wants a clearer accounting from the whole group, the third day may be structured to provide prioritization and action planning based on the previous discussions.

How short can an Open Space be?

Practitioners of Open Space are loath to call anything less than one full day "Open Space." However, some people are experimenting with shorter versions. We tried out a "mini–Open Space" in our workshops to give people a feel for what happens. Much to our delight, it works rather well in a three-hour block. This provides time for the traditional opening agenda setting, two forty-five-minute sessions, and some discussion. In *Tales from Open Space* (Owen, 1995, pp. 114–119), Larry Peterson describes three occasions where he used a mini–Open Space: (1) in a $3^1/_2$-hour planning committee meeting for a community event; (2) at the end of a three-day board retreat to discuss the work of the board for the next year, where he found that it revived flagging energy; and (3) the last afternoon and next morning (overnight) of a three-day meeting of the governing board of a national church body to develop proposals for action for the next year, which was followed by a decision-making meeting.

In the same volume, Anne Morgan Stadler suggests that some minimum conditions must be met for these "partial" Open Spaces. First, a clear work focus has to exist. Second, people need to take responsibility for their own participation and action. She contrasts this with brainstorming, where people creatively generate ideas that *others* can do. Finally, she believes that people must be open to new outcomes. The field must be open, not prescribed (Owen, 1995, p. 144).

We find her hypotheses very interesting as a guide. In our experience, the short experience shifts energy and engages people when it is used at the right moment. But it is clearly not the same as a three-day event around an intensely complex theme, where people may at first become confused, then struggle and emerge with new insights. The short event is, in our experience, more like a "free university" training design that allows a diverse agenda and the development of working interest groups.

Part Four Summary

Comparison of Methods

The table in this summary presents a straightforward comparison of the methods presented in Part Four, which involve the whole system in participative problem solving and decision making. As we show in the table, they address a variety of outcomes. An interesting variety of decision-making processes are also available to choose from. Generally, these methods are not limited to the smaller of the large groups (40 to 80 people). They all can accommodate over 100 people.

Finally, most of these methods use standard formats that accommodate many types of outcomes. The exception consists of Large Scale Interactive Events, which are designed for each client based on the outcomes desired and the state of the system at the time of the intervention.

Part Four Summary Table. Comparison: Large Group Methods for Whole-System Participative Work.

Method	Outcomes	Design Format	Decision-Making Process	Numbers
Simu-Real	Whole-system learning, problem sensing and solving, trying out new structures or processes	Action-reflection format	Choice made in advance • Advisory to management • Identified group • Participative	50 to 150
Work-Out	Problem-solving, process improvement	Standard framework, emergent content	Management decides in response to employee proposals	20 to 200
Open Space Technology	System-wide issue generation and exploration	Standard framework, emergent content	Not integral to the method (a prioritization and decision-making process may be added)	50 to 500
Large Scale Interactive Events	Intra- or inter-organizational coordination, training, problem solving	Standard activities selected and modified to client needs	Participative	50 to 1,000+

Part Five

Group Dynamics,
New Directions, and
How to Move Ahead

In this final part, we consider three important but different topics. In Chapter Fourteen, we describe the dynamics of large groups. Because the common element in these innovations is their large group setting, understanding the particular processes associated with large groups is imperative.

In Chapter Fifteen, we take up two topics. First, we describe the current modifications in large group methods and the interesting new directions in which practitioners are taking them. Then we discuss the underlying principles and values that we think cross all these new ways of working. This chapter provides guidance about the essential elements that are fundamental to the effective use of these methods.

Chapter Fourteen

Large Group Dynamics

Are the psychological processes of large groups different from those in small groups? We invite you to think for a few minutes about the following questions:

- How do you feel when you are a participant in a very large meeting (two hundred to three hundred people)?
- What are some of your concerns or fears?
- Is your behavior different from your typical behavior in small groups?

In the three-day seminar that we give on large group interventions, we begin our consideration of large group dynamics by asking participants to consider these questions privately. Then, everyone forms a fifty- to sixty-person seated circle, and we ask them to become a large group for half an hour and explore the dynamics that are present. No two sessions are ever alike, but we always find evidence of three issues that we believe it is critical to understand in order to work in large group settings.

The Dilemma of Voice

Large groups are, by definition, too large for people to have face-to-face interaction. In small groups of up to about a dozen people, each person has a reasonable chance to speak, be listened to, and be responded to. In small group dynamics, the expression "airtime" means the amount of time available for speaking. In an hour-long meeting of eight people, each person has about 7¹/₂ minutes for speaking. In such small groups, problems with speaking are not created by too little airtime. However, large groups have a structural airtime dilemma. Consider a group with fifty people who are in a meeting for 30 minutes. Each person can have just over half a minute. This means that she or he might be able to say a short sentence or two, but conversation and responding to others is not possible. Of course, that is not what happens. In large groups, typically, some people say quite a lot while others are silent.

This is the first major issue of large group dynamics. We are calling it *the dilemma of voice* (see also Main, 1975, and Menzies, 1960). We use the word *dilemma* here as Glidewell (1970) uses it to describe a situation that cannot be changed or permanently resolved. Problems can be solved. Dilemmas, like even a good marriage, have to be lived with! In social settings, most people from individualistic countries like ours want to be recognized as individuals who have worth and a unique contribution to make. In a small group, we do this through our verbal contributions. We *individuate* ourselves by what we say in the group. People get to know us and what we can contribute. Through interaction, groups develop patterns of roles and members rely on each other.

In a large group, however, people always have the problem of feeling recognized, because it is difficult to get an opportunity to speak. This is a structural difficulty created by the time available and the number of people who want to use it. In addition, the sheer number of other people who are present is intimidating to some, especially those who prefer one-to-one interaction. Even those who do speak in large groups will not be able to know the reactions of others as easily as when fewer people are present.

For some, large groups are a challenge and they rise to it by trying to make themselves known. This can lead to a situation in which a few people do much of the speaking while others experience "the tyranny of the few." Resentments can grow because often the "big talkers" have taken on their role without having others offer it to them. Those who remain silent take on the role of quiet participant.

It is easy for them to grow more and more passive and to feel more and more marginal to the group. Then, when they do have something to say, it is hard to break out of the passive role and speak.

One partial explanation for this phenomenon that comes from research on small groups is "diffusion of responsibility" (Latane and Darley, 1976). The idea is that as numbers increase, the personal sense of responsibility for the outcomes of the group decreases and this affects behavior. People in large groups are less likely to act when they see an occasion that calls for action. National attention focused on this phenomenon in the Kitty Genovese incident in New York City in 1964, when thirty-seven people stood by and did nothing while a woman was attacked and killed. The response by social psychologists was a flurry of research that focused on the processes that cause people to act even when they have something at risk (theories of altruism) and the processes that cause people not to act when others are in need (theories of deindividuation) (Zimbardo, 1970).

What do these large group events do to cope with this problem of individuation? Can people feel active and able to contribute in events with over five hundred participants? The genius of the methods in this book is that even in very large events, people spend much of their time in small groups doing specific tasks. In the search methods, the ICA Strategic Planning Process, all of the work design methods, and Real Time Strategic Change, the table group has structured interaction. Often, explicit directions call for everyone to have a minute or two to give his or her views before any discussion. The functional group roles of facilitator, recorder, reporter, and timekeeper are rotated for every new task so that everyone gets active and assumes responsibility. In the general sessions of the whole event, tables report out and ask questions so that each group has a voice. Dot voting, a process in which the participants each have a few sticky, colored dots to place on wall charts for the items they believe are most important, also individuates people.

Simu-Real individuates people by placing them in their known work groups. Open Space accomplishes this by declaring people to be responsible for their own experience. It encourages them to be active and responsible about their own learning and goals, either by proposing what they want to do or by managing themselves so that they do not disengage. In other words, underlying the effectiveness of these large group events is the use of small group technology and processes that allow people to participate fully and feel engaged.

The Dilemma of Structure in Large Groups

If you have ever been in a crowd that was out of control or that was being harassed by onlookers or the police, you know some of the hidden fears that many people carry about large groups. They may fear that things will get out of control and that violence will occur. Experience with tense situations in groups varies. For some people, any perceived tension threatens violence. Others can be aware of tension before they become worried. When I (Barbara) lived in New York City in the 1960s, I occasionally went to events in a theater on the Lower East Side that was known for sometimes becoming violent. I always went with experienced friends who could judge the level of tension, and they left before anybody got hurt. I could not make those judgments—any tension scared me.

Another fear in large groups is of potential chaos and total disorganization. How can so many people get organized and get something done? It could be bedlam! Thus, anxiety is always incipient in any large group situation. People and cultures differ in their response to these forces. Some people and some cultures tolerate more degrees of ambiguity than others.

Structure has the capacity to "bind" anxiety. It organizes experience and gives it coherence and meaning. Agendas, job descriptions, or organizational charts create a sense, at least symbolically, of order and purpose. The right amount of structure is reassuring and allows people to function in a healthy way. The dilemma is that we do not know how much anxiety exists and how much structure is needed. The paradox is that *too little structure* in a situation where more is needed will increase anxiety and is likely to produce acting out (jargon for behavior that alleviates anxiety rather than reaching objectives). In the same way, *too much structure* in situations that need less will also increase anxiety and lead to acting out. So figuring out how much structure is needed is like walking a tightwire—it is possible to fall off on either side.

I (Barbara) learned this lesson in an indelible experience in the late 1970s. That was the year I agreed to be chair of the Social Sciences Policy Committee at the State University of New York at Buffalo, where I teach. I thought it would be a routine committee, with not much work. Then, in early spring, a major retrenchment was proposed by the administration that would have caused some social science departments to lay off tenured professors. Nothing in academia makes faculty more anxious than the threat of losing the tenure system. In the 1970s, the thought was intolerable to most faculty, and feelings were running very high. I was barraged by demands to call a meeting of the social science faculty, a group of about two hundred. I realized that we would have to meet and my heart sank. I remembered previous faculty meetings that had disintegrated into shouting matches. People got angry and nothing much got done. I was scared that this meeting would get out of hand in the same way.

Then I remembered the rule of thumb about too little or too much structure from my Tavistock training and ideas began to fall into place. I was aware that the campus was awash with rumors but very little hard data about what really was going on. I decided that the first structure we needed was a shared data base from people close to the sources of power. I structured the two-hour meeting, scheduled in the school cafeteria, to open with thirty minutes of informational input from very knowledgeable people and questions for clarification only. Then I asked everyone who wanted to propose some action or make a resolution to bring these ideas forward so that everyone in the room could know the agenda. Finally, I suggested that we work on the agenda items in order. I proposed this very simple structure at the opening of the meeting and asked for support in staying with it. There was agreement, and although people pushed the boundaries at some points, most people's desire to see something useful happen helped me to maintain both the plan and order in the room. After two hours of heated debate, we had passed several resolutions and taken substantial action. The feeling in the room at the end of the meeting was fatigue coupled with elation. We had acted as a body and we had a plan.

To my great surprise and inward amusement, for a month after that meeting I was treated like some kind of campus celebrity. Every time I would see colleagues in the hall or parking lot, they would say things like "I don't know how you did it!" "What did you do? It was magic!" "I can't believe we had a meeting where we actually got something accomplished!" They attributed some magical skill to me. On the other hand, it was crystal-clear to me that without my understanding of the relationship between anxiety and structure, I would have had no theory to guide my actions in planning that meeting.

As we have seen in the chapters on each model, many of these large group events provide clear task structure but encourage active and individually determined participation. At times, chaos threatens, but enough structure is in place to provide guidance. For example, after the technical analysis in work design methods, participants may be overwhelmed by all that is wrong and all that needs to be done. The next steps in the process enable them to select the most important priorities to inform their decisions about change. Or, in another example, in Future Search, participants may be overwhelmed by all the data they initially create. When each table gets a data-analysis task and these reports are then integrated, a workable way of structuring is provided. The rotating roles at tables also create a group structure that helps the task along but does not cast anyone in a dominant role. People are never in a group with their boss and are usually with people from other parts of the organization, so some organizational constraints against being open are reduced.

The Egocentric Dilemma

Employees' views of their organization are colored by their experience in their unit and the role that they carry. We each know only the most immediate part of the blind man's elephant. When the whole organization gathers in a large group, many people are unaware of the limitations of their organizational view. They believe that their view of things is accurate. The *egocentric dilemma* is the situation that obtains at the beginning of the large group event, when hundreds of people with differing pictures of organizational reality all act as if theirs is the only true reality.

In the same way that students who dislike the textbook in my (Barbara's) organizational psychology course are stunned to discover that other students really like it and find it interesting, so, in organizations, the people on the shop floor are surprised by the views of the people in Marketing and vice versa. We look at the world through our own experience, egocentrically, often not appreciating the differences between us.

When the whole organization comes together in one place and begins to talk, people have the possibility of beginning to see things from other perspectives. The majority of methods assign people to heterogeneous max-mix groups for substantial amounts of time. Open Space and Work-Out cluster people around interests in specific issues. In these groups, people share views and begin to understand what it is like to be in different organizational roles. They also see the organization whole rather than partially.

The Contagion of Affect

The seminal contribution of Bion (1961) to our understanding of group life, the role of the unconscious affective dimensions that he calls "sentience," helps us to understand how these affective forces can impede or further the primary task of the group.

What happens as groups get larger? One of the earliest works in social psychology, LeBon's study (1986) of the crowd, also empha-sizes how affect flows in larger groups. The simplest way to say it is that affect, like colds, can be caught. In other words, people begin to experience feelings because they feel them vicariously in others, not because they are all having the same experience. In large groups, this has serious implications. On the upside, Mardi Gras and other large crowd revelries are places where positive affect spreads. On the downside, Zimbardo (1970) demonstrated that people can join together in violent self-reinforcing cycles in groups.

The tone or affective center of large groups can be manipulated because affect is contagious. Politicians know this only too well. You can see it happening on national television when the political conventions are in session. It also happens in organizations, espe-cially when not enough information is available for employees to make rational sense of what is happening. Secrecy and impending layoffs send waves of fear and rumors throughout organizations, often in the face of other information that is not trusted. The pos-sibility of swirling affect is present in all large groups.

Affective contagion in a large group setting can be seen when people who have clearly had quite different experiences all profess the same emotion. In a debriefing of an outdoor "ropes" experience, we once watched forty people, who an hour before were clearly enjoying themselves and enthusiastically trying to get their entire group over a high wall, "catch" the negative affect of a very few members who were angry and upset about their own performance. In a few minutes, the entire group was describing the experience as "awful and a waste of time."

The potential for affective contagion in large groups has two implications. One concerns structure. Small groups interacting within the large group substantially reduce the probability of con-tagion. The second concerns professional facilitation. People who plan and manage large group events need to be trained and com-fortable in dealing with a range of very strong feelings, as well as in understanding how affect can operate in these settings. This is a sophisticated competence that is developed over time with continued training. In other words, it is not one-shot or one-workshop learning! Good sources of experiential training in these dynamics are the programs of the A. K. Rice Institute. (See the Appendix.)

Chapter Fifteen

Current Innovations
and Underlying Values

The final chapter of this book has two purposes. The first is to share the latest innovations that we see emerging and developing as more organizations and communities use these large-scale methods and adapt them to their particular situations.

The second part of this chapter grows out of our attempts to synthesize all that we have read, heard about, and experienced over the past five years. Our purpose here will be to answer our own questions about the key principles and values that underlie all of the methods presented in the book. We hope that this discussion will give our readers a touchstone, a place to ground themselves, even as they use these methods or develop their own unique innovations.

Current Innovations:
What Is Happening to the Methods?

As internal or external consultants start to use these large-scale approaches, it is inevitable that adaptations and mutations will occur. Unique circumstances, special purposes, the nature of the audience, different cultural settings, and the inevitable refining of the methods as they are used over time often result in changes to the basic approach. These areas of work are emergent, often developing in several different directions at the same time. Fortunately, because people share their work at conferences, mutual influencing occurs.

In talking with the originators of the methods described in this book, we clearly saw that in addition to the changes that evolve through the conferences, the originators themselves are continually discovering and evolving new ways of doing things and new methods for dealing with the special needs and purposes of the client system. We are writing this book at a given point in time, but we know that, even as we write, new developments are occurring. For example, in the original design of Future Search, representatives from each group would take future scenarios, find common themes, then report these findings back to the group at large. The result was that in the workshop, people lost ownership; this created resistance to the themes that were put forward. By using these experiences to fine-tune the Future Search method, consultants began to include the whole group in discovering the common themes from the scenarios.

Another innovation that is occurring is the use of basic design elements from these large-scale events in half-day or one-day meetings that deal with an organizational issue, usually one that has more to do with the daily running of the business than with the creation of a new direction or a redesign of the work structure. The following are a few examples of how people in leading-edge organizations are working with the concept of "getting everyone in the room" to deal with organizational issues.

An airline's human resource department was designing a new performance appraisal system. The department had ideas and information, including a draft of categories of behaviors that employees would be evaluated on, as well as survey data about the performance system. The department did not rest on that information, however. They wanted and needed feedback to crucial questions, such as "Are these the right or key behaviors that people should be evaluated on?" and "Are the questions to elicit data about those behaviors clear and unambiguous?"

To get this feedback, the department involved managers, supervisors, and employees, all of whom would be required to use the new system or have it used on them, to help determine the behaviors on which people would be evaluated. They brought together several hundred people and used a combination of mixed groups (nobody with her or his own boss) and functional area groupings. Not only did the human resource department come away with valuable input and modification of some of their original work; they came up with new behavioral categories that were more appropriate to the current business environment. In addition, the new system this one-day event helped to create was much easier to implement because people were willing to support what they themselves had been able to influence.

In another company, a small financial institution, management set up a series of task forces to work on different organizational issues. The internal consultant believed that, despite all the task-force activity, nothing much was happening. Some groups were stymied, waiting for others to finish their work. Other task forces felt that they should be merged with another group. One group felt that they had no real purpose and should be eliminated. Almost all felt that the deadlines were totally unrealistic.

With the approval of the CEO, the internal consultant called a half-day meeting with all three-hundred task-force members. Using a giant wall chart to map out the information, all the participants addressed deliverables, sequencing, time frames, mergers, and eliminations. This meeting was so successful that everyone agreed to hold regular meetings in which task forces would report back, receive feedback and suggestions, and determine when joint meetings with another group might be beneficial.

Another example comes from a pharmaceutical company that had created more than ten task forces to make recommendations about the process flow for developing new drug products. Here the problem was overlapping roles and lack of clarity about the goals for each group. A one-day large group involving all members of the task forces was very helpful in clarifying roles, straightening out goals, and eliminating overlaps.

After using this large-scale approach for redesign, stakeholders in a manufacturing organization decided to bring in suppliers and customers each quarter to share information and address issues and changes. In addition, at a recent large-scale change meeting in Dallas, The Boeing Company reported that its managers often call a half-day meeting of several hundred people from different functions to work on cross-functional issues that are getting in the way of the work.

Instead of sending out an employee climate survey, a small financial institution invited three hundred employees from different levels and functions to participate in a one-day "climate discussion." In mixed roundtable groups, the employees discussed questions that would normally have been part of a written survey, then gave table reports on the questions and their responses to them. The human resource people felt that the quality of the information about employee reactions was far superior to anything a survey could produce. They also believed that it provided an impetus for change. At the end of the meeting, managers and employees reported how much they had learned, and one employee later said that the conversations across levels actually created a change in their culture. We agree and think that an actual change in the organizational climate occurred, resulting in improved relations among all organizational levels.

A consultant who works with churches that are looking for a new pastor has used a shortened version of Future Search just before involving the parish in developing criteria for hiring the new pastor. The congregation explores its history, the current reality (both internal and external), and the future purpose and vision they see for their church, given the "diagnosis" of its environment. After this exploration, the parish looks at the implications of this process for calling a new pastor, such as the qualifications and skills they require, not only for the pastor but also for themselves.

These are only a few of the many possible applications, and there are more to come! The art form, of course, is recognizing the opportunity to use them in ongoing organizational life.

The Use of Information Systems Technology for Large Group Events

Another important development is the increased use of information technology for large group events. We believe that this will happen in two areas: (1) software that will facilitate teams in these large group events in generating ideas and prioritizing their thinking and (2) use of interactive networks such as E-mail or the Internet for large group events held in remote locations. Using these technologies, people from across the United States could gather to discuss the topics and share with each other their thoughts and insights, all without leaving their homes or offices. Videoconferencing could also be used, although this particular technology currently carries a hefty price tag.

Many companies have already begun to meet this information challenge. For example, Metasystems in Washington, D.C., is using the Internet to help teachers converse about curricular changes. Co-Vision in San Francisco, along with a number of other companies, has developed software to facilitate brainstorming and handle prioritizing tasks in large group events. Their methodology was demonstrated recently at the Organization Development Network annual meeting. A more modest but very effective approach was used by the Canadian government's human resource department. Regional human resource groups got together to discuss topics proposed by the central office. After discussions in each region, the participants contributed their ideas by conference call. All parties were on the line and able to make decisions, without having to travel to the main office.

Because of the cost of air and other travel, we will continue to see very inventive technological ways of involving people in participative planning.

From Event to Organizational Culture Change

Boeing, Blue Shield of California, General Electric, Hewlett-Packard, and Syncrude are using these methods not just to generate energy and for redesign but as a way of running their business. Because these meetings cease to be "special events," employees and managers feel free to call cross-functional meetings of key stakeholders to address work-related issues.

For example, at Syncrude, which had been engaged for some time in Participative Design, confusion arose between what was a technician's role and what was a supervisor's role. The parties involved called a meeting, got together, and worked it out on their own. The Boeing Company adopted large group methods for designing the 777. For the first time, they involved customers in the design process. Phil Condit, Boeing CEO, describes how they set up design build teams composed of engineering, manufacturing, tool making, marketing, and finance. Frequent all-team meetings kept employees informed (Public Broadcasting Service, 1994).

The capacity to do this comes from cultural change brought about by sustained involvement in these critical-mass events. Asking people to work together and build cross-functional, cross-level relationships increases their capability, as soon as an issue is identified, to find the right people and engage them in working on the issue. These methods are actually creating more self-managing systems within organizations. The culture created by such methods is what was envisioned when people began adopting ideas such as Total Quality Management (TQM) and team-based work environments. What is different, we feel, is that these whole-system organizational methods have a greater chance of changing the underlying system of an organization and breaking down the old nondemocratic structures that often inhibit the TQM and team-building approaches.

Jack Welch, CEO of General Electric, talks about boundaryless organizations (Tichy and Sherman, 1993). As he is well aware, the greatest potential for problems exists where transactions move across boundaries, whether internal or external. We do not believe that boundaries will totally disappear, but taking the initiative to bring people together to work the boundary issues is one of the many important outcomes of adopting and using large group methods.

Underlying Principles and Values

As we have learned about and been deeply immersed in these methods over the last five years, we have asked, "What underlies all the methods? What are the fundamental assumptions they hold in common? What is really key to their being effective?" Here are our nominations for the underlying principles and values that all these methods share. We believe that these principles can be used to evaluate whether large group methods are appropriate and will be very helpful in the planning process.

Valuing Engagement

Underlying the methods in this book is a bone-deep belief in participation—a fundamental conviction that when people have the important information about a system and are allowed to become collaboratively and fully engaged with others around these issues, they become highly motivated to take responsibility for change and improvement.

As our awareness of participation as a value in a democratic society has grown, we have become increasingly worried about the use of these methods where this value is absent. If the methods are used simply to come up with a stamp of approval on an already-decided management decision, they will backfire. People know when they are being manipulated. Many organizations have a history of management's using the newest theory of organization development or design to railroad employees into what management thinks is best, without ever consulting the employees. This is why employees often come to these events, at least at the start, with what we consider a "healthy" degree of distrust. If the decision makers do not share in the value of participation, fear loss of control, or are unwilling to trust in the goodwill latent in their people, these methods should not be employed.

Even though management is often seen as a major roadblock to change in an organization, our experience shows that most people in management positions think quite differently. They are constantly searching for ways to bring people on board and aligned behind a vision that is crucial to the ongoing business of the company. They understand that it is their job to get everyone pulling in one direction, and they are constantly looking for new and better ways to do it. What they have lacked, until this point, is not the desire but a method for consistently getting this change accomplished. Figure 15.1 describes how the participatory process works and how it leads to more active system involvement in decision making.

Selecting the Right Issue

Many meetings and conferences fail because the issue or purpose is unclear, too broad, or too narrowly focused. In large group work, the issue needs to be systemic, cutting across all levels of the organization and across all spectrums of stakeholders, both internal and external. The issue must be important enough so that a critical mass of people has information to share on the subject as well as a strong desire to influence it. In addition, these events should be seen as part of a long-term change process, not just as isolated, one-shot events.

At a Future Search Conference that I (Billie) did in a small city in Connecticut (also mentioned in Chapter Four), the presenting issue was violence. As the planning group talked together, they arrived at the following purpose for the conference: "Building a Community Free from Fear." The title meant something to the community: it focused the issue on what they most desired. More than 125 people signed up to come on two weekdays in June! Of course, lowering the level of violent crime was important, but this broader purpose helped the group to move from simply controlling violence to supporting and strengthening the community and its members.

Figure 15.1. How the Participatory Process Works.

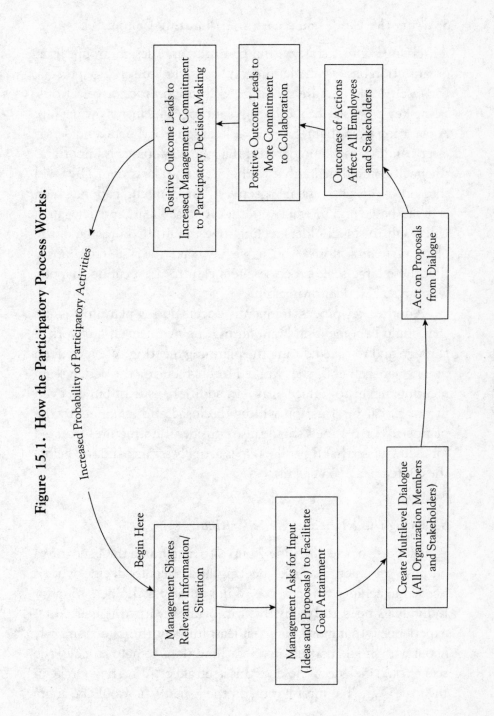

Starting the Conference with the Planning Committee

All change efforts start with a planning and design group. If an organization has begun planning, it has started the change process, because people are already engaged in important conversations. Some key processes occur during planning. The first is ownership. A planning team that represents at least some of the stakeholders is essential. If the stakeholders feel that the conference is important, they will communicate that to their stakeholder group. They will share ideas, insights, and perspectives. This communication, which is broad-based and interactive rather than set apart and delegated, will result in stakeholders feeling invested in the outcome of the planning team's efforts. And, as we have said, the systemic changes that these large-scale processes are meant to assist cannot happen without stakeholder ownership.

Another key process frequently occurs during planning: issues that could become a problem during the event itself are worked through and resolved during the planning meeting. We have seen union-management issues worked through during the design team meeting, never to surface again. In addition, as trust builds, even more critical information will be disclosed and available to the planners. The planners should also consider the structures required for follow-up so that the follow-up is actually set into motion before the conference even begins.

Selecting the Right People Is Critical

A major task of the planning group is to help frame the issue into a purpose statement for the meeting and then to decide who is needed to achieve this purpose. What other stakeholder groups or individuals need to be involved in dealing with this issue? Our experience is that most groups, at least initially, think too narrowly about who should participate. Some questions to help broaden the scope could include: Who does this issue affect? Who has a stake in the issue? Who has information on the issue? Who would be angry if they were not invited? Whose influence and perspective are important? One useful exercise to generate ideas is to put the issue in the center of the page and draw spokes out to smaller circles, which represent potential stakeholders in the issue. It is best to err on the side of being inclusive rather than exclusive.

We know several organizations and groups that expanded their ideas of who should participate, with excellent results. In one case, a school system holding a meeting about an educational issue invited a taxpayer organization—usually considered the enemy— to the meeting. Through dialogue and realization of common ground and goals, the school system turned an "enemy" into a supporter. In another case (discussed in Chapter Four), a university that was redesigning an MBA program brought in not only faculty and administration but also current MBA students, alumni who had graduated from the program and been "out in the world" for a number of years, and members of the business community, who had significant input about what kind of skills they were looking for in MBA graduates. All of these parties, who were traditionally considered separate, were brought together and produced rich, dynamic dialogue about the future of the program.

We think that it is important to include a negative example, as well. Another educational organization, a religious seminary, decided that they wanted to conduct a Future Search conference to help them see through and beyond some divisive internal issues. However, they chose not to bring in external stakeholders. Thus, there were no "tie-breakers" at the meetings, no input from outside the already well-worn circles of internal conflict. The result was that the same old dynamics were replayed. For this organization, bringing in outside stakeholders would not have magically solved the internal problems, but the outsiders' perceptions and feedback might have enabled the insiders to get out of the "fight" mode and move on to addressing issues that were being avoided.

In selecting the right people to be present, it is also important for the decision makers to be present and visible. Recommendations that go to some steering committee or to senior managers rarely get fully implemented or succeed. Unless the decision makers are there, participating in the process, it becomes disempowering. We heard about one Future Search Conference, at a state government organization, that was conducted without the top brass being present. When the recommendations of the conference were presented, the leadership ignored them, creating more feelings of alienation and distrust than were present before the conference. All the participants' efforts and expectations were destroyed, and they felt as if they had been manipulated. One of the outcomes of these whole-system events must be the assumption of responsibility for the future by *everyone*. This enables the organization to change in real time.

Structuring for Good Conversations

Another key design ingredient is making sure that meaningful conversations take place. These good conversations need to occur in mixed groups at tables, in stakeholder groups with sources (customers, suppliers, regulators) who bring information, and in the larger group. The goal is to help people to recognize multiple perspectives. Of course, we talk about helping people to recognize multiple perspectives as a given, but our experience is that during table discussions, even when a table has visible diversity, participants are usually astounded to discover that not everyone sees a particular issue in the same way.

As participants talk to one another, often to people in the organization they have never talked with before, they become aware of their own filters and the value of different viewpoints. They step back and look at the issue from another point of view and become less egocentric. They learn, they feel challenged, and they become engaged. They find common ground and build a common data base because they are forced to reconcile different viewpoints and integrate ideas and purposes. So, for example, when a table puts together its three or four questions or statements for consideration by the community, it will have integrated the different responses of the members at the table. The table responses and questions have been thought through and discussed, and the responses tend to be far superior in quality to eight different unintegrated responses, which may simply represent people's "hot buttons." Out of these processes emerges a richness of perspectives, a whole that is more than the sum of its parts.

For this drawing out and integrating of different perspectives to work, the questions groups will be addressing and how that information will be shared, organized, and prioritized must be carefully planned. Allow time for table interactions around the data. It may seem incidental, but we have found that having five-foot-diameter round tables with eight people to a table stimulates interaction. Once, when we were doing some work in England, we insisted that participants sit at this type of table. The people in charge of logistics thought we were crazy but gave in to our requirements. After the conference, they commented that they had never achieved the degree of interaction and excitement in previous meetings that they had with these mixed-group, five-foot-diameter round tables. We would like to think that some of this was the result of our work with the group, and perhaps it was. What we are sure about is that our English friends quickly ordered five-foot-diameter round tables for all their meeting rooms.

The final point in structuring for good conversations is also one of most important issues in our world (not just in organizations). This is the issue of *voice*. Giving people a voice is a key value in all these methods. And part of giving people a voice is allowing the multiple voices to engage in dialogue, to converse, and to search for meaning with each other. We believe that out of these conversations can come innovative ideas, constructive approaches, and new commitments to the organization or community.

Allowing Time for Reflection and Creative Breakthroughs

Our culture is short-term and fast-moving; therefore, these processes need to compensate for our strong cultural bias toward "making it happen" and must create time for reflection or, as Marv Weisbord calls it, "soak time." During these meetings and events, people need time to take in enormous amounts of information, think about them, and talk about them, without feeling pushed into knee-jerk decisions. Of course, many employees have been guilty of allowing management to pressure them into accomplishing tasks in fewer hours than they need, in one day instead of three. We are convinced, however, that it is important to push back and allow sufficient time for people to reflect on issues that have been generated.

One of the consultants who used Open Space Technology in Canada reports that she ran a very effective Open Space with the same group for three days but allowed a day in between day one and day two and again between day two and day three to give the participants a chance to absorb what they had learned during the first day. We do not know or understand all of the mind's unconscious processes, but a substantial body of research supports the fact that major breakthroughs occur when people work hard for a while, then take a break (other work or recreation) and allow the subconscious to work its magic.

Planning Turning Points: From "Me" to "We"

In the paradigm shifts that occur in these meetings, people suddenly see the world differently. As they share more information, they see the whole, not just a part. What are the elements in the methods that build toward this shift?

Almost all of these methods encourage a diagnosis of the current state and a process by which the group takes responsibility for what has happened and what needs to happen. When the entire group takes responsibility, finger pointing disappears. When all information and perspectives are out in the open, and when people see how the parts of the organization interact and how these interactions affect performance, then it is possible to change and to manage the interactions differently. In Future Search, this shift from "me" to "we" often occurs during the "prouds and sorries." In Real Time Strategic Change, different exercises in several places create this movement from "my issue, my department" to "this is our organization or community." The ownership shifts to the whole and makes real improvement and change possible.

In the organizational redesign methods, this shift often becomes palpable as participants analyze the work flow. Looking at the whole process, often for the first time, they recognize the many "glitches" that have been allowed to continue. In the ICA Strategic Planning Process, the shift becomes evident when the community analyzes and interprets its own data, touches those data, discusses what they mean, and discovers the contradictions to the vision. As those contradictions are further probed for root causes, the group takes ownership and becomes invested in the whole. They want to make it work, become intrigued as the challenge of making it work emerges, and move from a self-centered perspective to one centered in the whole.

Building In an Opportunity for the "If"

As Herb Shepherd, one of the founders of the field of organization development, once noted, people agree more on the future than they ever do on the present or past. Many of the change methods discussed in this book build into the design an opportunity for the group to create a vision of a preferred future. They might ask, "What would we like to see happening in our organization five years in the future?" or "What would the future look like if everything in the organization was working at its best?" Different methods use different names: ideal futures, practical vision, the preferred future. No matter what they are called, the "if" that is built into all of these methods asks participants to dream about what they would like the future to look like, what would be their best hope. The stretch between the current reality (where we are now) and the vision of the future (where we would like to be) creates a tension that can produce action and commitment.

We must note that because phrases such as "generating vision" and "seeing the future" have been overused and sometimes misused, they may turn people off. In that case, try building an opportunity for the "if" by asking the question another way: "If things were working at their best, what would be happening?" Moving to the results people would like to see reframes the issue, encouraging broader perspectives and fresh approaches.

Allowing Opportunities for Efficacy and Commitment

We have used phrases such as "exerting influence" or "feeling empowered," but we like the word *efficacious*. People need to feel efficacious, that is, having the capacity to adequately produce a desired effect. All these methods have built into them numerous opportunities for people to be efficacious, by analyzing and interpreting information, setting priorities, creating new approaches, and developing action plans. A good question to ask in reviewing and then choosing a design is "Have we built into this design opportunities for people to influence, to feel effectual, to make a difference both individually and collaboratively?" All of these models build in an opportunity for people to commit to the process of change. As they begin to feel that they can influence a change process and its outcome, they start committing to making real what they have only dreamed about before. And they begin searching for ways to support and make a public commitment to that change.

Using the Zamboni Principle

One of the less obvious but essential elements in running large group events is having an effective infrastructure—that is, good logistics. Even though most participants will not be conscious of this infrastructure, they would certainly notice and, possibly, be distracted if it were not in place. Thus it is crucial to make sure that these events run seamlessly—no glitches, no ruts, no unexpected bumps—just like the ice at the skating rink after the Zamboni has gone by.

It is essential to consider, well ahead of time, logistics such as room size, table and chair layout, room lighting, the audiovisual and microphone systems, the pace of the tasks and the clarity with which they are laid out, and the way the food is served. The Appendix includes resource books with excellent discussions of logistics.

In the End, What Really Counts?

It is not the events that comprise the change process but the change process itself that counts. Knowing the core principles is the first step in deciding if an organization can support this type of change process. Selecting a systemic issue and getting started by planning is next. Getting the whole system into the room, structuring the meetings for good conversation, and allowing time for creative reflection are crucial to generating ideas and perspectives, moving from the "me" to the "we," and allowing people to dream and to feel purposeful and efficacious.

But to get meaningful, long-term results instead of quick-fix, short-term ones, organizations need a process—an implementation structure—to support and manage change. That is what this book is about. As we have explored these methods, we have come to realize that the process *is* the message. Selecting the right issue is important, but the process by which we engage people around that issue is what communicates a different way of developing an organizational culture and doing business. Issues—the "what"—will always be around. More important is the process, the methods we use to get the issues addressed.

Appendix

Part One: An Introduction to Large Group Interventions

A Brief History of Large Group Interventions

A two-and-one-half-day public workshop on the methods in this book run by Alban and Bunker three times each year (also available for groups within organizations). For more information, contact Conference Support Systems, Northwood, NH. Phone: 603–942–8189, fax: 603–942–8190.

Part Two: The Methods: Creating the Future Together

The Search Conference

Emery, M., and Purser, R. E. (1996). *The Search Conference: Theory and practice.* San Francisco: Jossey-Bass.

A theory-based guide to Search Conferences including business and community case examples. A methodology section includes information on planning, designing, and managing a Search Conference.

Training

Merrelyn Emery offers five-day training courses in the Search Conference and Participative Design through the University of New Mexico at Las Cruces several times a year. Phone: 505–646–1821.

Future Search

Weisbord, M. R. (1987). *Productive workplaces: Organizing and managing for dignity, meaning, and community.* San Francisco: Jossey-Bass.

The history and theory that led up to the development of ideas about improving the whole system. This was the first statement of the importance of getting the whole system in the room, with a description of an early case.

Weisbord, M. R. (1992). *Discovering common ground.* San Francisco: Berrett-Koehler.

A good description of the Future Search Conference and its underlying core values and principles. Most of the book consists of cases from both the public and private sectors.

Weisbord, M. R., and Janoff, S. (1995). *Future Search.* San Francisco: Berrett-Koehler.

A comprehensive guide on how to do Future Search Conferences. It includes handouts, charts, and other specifics.

Videos

Search for quality. (1992). Blue Sky Productions, Philadelphia, PA.

A Future Search at Hayworth, Inc., an office furniture manufacturer in Holland, MI. Two versions: 26 minutes and 12 minutes. Phone: 800–358–0022.

Discovering community. (1996). Blue Sky Productions. Philadelphia, PA.

A Future Search in Santa Cruz County, California. 45 minutes. Phone: 800–358–0022.

Other Resources

SearchNet is a membership organization that publishes a newsletter and other materials about the work of Future Search practitioners. Members pay an annual fee and agree to do one pro bono Future Search a year. Address: 4333 Kelly Drive, Philadelphia, PA 19129. Phone: 215–951–0300, fax: 215–951–0313. Training is also offered by SearchNet several times a year.

Real Time Strategic Change

Dannemiller, K., and Jacobs, R. W. (1992). Changing the way organizations change: A revolution in common sense. *Journal of Applied Behavioral Science, 28,* 480–498.

Jacobs, R. W. (1994). *Real Time Strategic Change.* San Francisco: Berrett-Koehler.

Principles and practices of Real Time Strategic Change. These two works include generic designs, cases and results, and comments by clients about their results and experience.

Dannemiller-Tyson Associates. (1994). *Real Time Strategic Change: A consultant's guide to large scale meetings.* Ann Arbor, MI: Author. Phone: 313–662–1330.

A comprehensive manual on planning, designing, and managing large-scale meetings. It includes a generic design, samples of actual designs, and an excellent section on logistics, as well as a sample registration packet, handouts, and evaluation forms (pricey, but worth it!).

Videos

No commercial videos are available, but Dannemiller-Tyson does have some films that clients have produced for internal use.

Training

Training is offered by Dannemiller-Tyson Associates several times a year. Phone: 313–662–1330. Robert Jacobs's firm, Five Oceans International, may also be contacted for information about training. Phone: 313–475–4215.

ICA Strategic Planning Process

Spencer, L. J. (1989). *Winning through participation.* Dubuque, IA: Kendall/Hunt.

A good description of the ICA Strategic Planning Process with a case example. Other methods of increasing group participation are also given.

Troxel, J. P. (1993). *Participation works: Business cases from around the world.* Alexandria, VA: Miles River Press.

Contains a series of cases from around the world, not all of which are large group events.

Training

Contact the Institute of Cultural Affairs, 4750 Sheridan Road, Chicago, IL 60640. Phone: 312–769–6363, fax: 312–769–1144.

Part Three: The Methods: Work Design

The Conference Model®

Axelrod, D. (1992). Getting everyone involved: How one organization involved its employees, supervisors and managers in redesigning the organization. *Journal of Applied Behavioral Science, 28*, 499–509.

Videos

Accelerated work redesign. (1993). Blue Sky Productions. Philadelphia, PA. 25 minutes. Phone: 800–358–0022.

Training

The Conference Model® Professional Skills Seminar Handbook is available as part of the training seminar offered several times each year by The Axelrod Group, 723 Laurel Avenue, Wilmette, IL 60091. Phone: 847–251–7361.

Fast Cycle Full Participation Work Design

Training

Pasmore, Fitz, and Frank and the Organization Redesign Institute offer several different workshops on organizational redesign. Registration is through Conference Support Systems, Northwood, NH. Phone: 603–942–8189, fax: 603–942–8190.

The *Fast Cycle Full Participation Facilitators Handbook* is available to participants attending the FCFP training workshop. Phone: 207–793–2600.

Real Time Work Design

Training
Call Dannemiller-Tyson Associates. Phone: 313–662–1330.

Participative Design

Cabana, S. (1995). Can people restructure their own work? *Target*, 11(6), 16–30.

Cabana, S. (1995). Participative Design works, partially participative doesn't. *Journal for Quality and Participation*, 18(1), 6–9.

Emery, F. (1995). Participative Design: Effective, flexible and successful, now! *Journal for Quality and Participation*, 18(1), 6–9.

Emery, M. (Ed.). (1993). Participative Design for participative democracy. Canberra, Australia: Australian National University, Centre for Continuing Education.

Training
Merrelyn Emery offers five-day training courses in Search Conference and Participative Design through the University of New Mexico at Las Cruces several times a year. Phone: 505–646–1821.

Part Four: The Methods: Whole-System Participative Work

Simu-Real

Klein, D. (1992). Simu-Real: A simulation approach to organizational change. *Journal of Applied Behavioral Science*, 28, 566–578.

Training
Call Conference Support Systems for information. Phone: 603–942–8189, fax: 603–942–8190.

Work-Out

Tichy, N., and Sherman, S. (1993). *Control your destiny or someone else will.* New York: Doubleday.

Open Space Technology

Owen, H. (1993). *Open Space Technology*. Potomac, MD: Abbott Press. Phone: 301–469–9269, fax: 301–983–9314.

A basic primer on Open Space, what to do, and how to do it.

Owen, H. (1995). *Tales from Open Space*. Potomac, MD: Abbott Press. Phone: 301–469–9269, fax: 301–983–9314.

Cases of Open Space practice in varied settings.

Training

Training is available regionally when organized by local groups. Information is usually available from Harrison Owen at 301–469–9269.

Part Five: Group Dynamics, New Directions, and How to Move Ahead

Large Group Dynamics

Training is available through the A. K. Rice Institute, P. O. Box 1776, Jupiter, FL 33468–1776. Phone: 561–744–1350.

References

Alinksy, S. (1946). *Reveille for radicals*. Chicago: University of Chicago Press.

Argyris, C. (1982). *Reasoning, learning, and action: Individual and organizational*. San Francisco: Jossey-Bass.

Axelrod, D. (1992). Getting everyone involved: How one organization involved its employees, supervisors and managers in redesigning the organization. *Journal of Applied Behavioral Science, 28*(4), 499–509.

Beckhard, R., and Harris, R. (1967). The confrontation meeting. *Harvard Business Review, 45*(2), 149–155.

Beckhard, R., and Harris, R. (1977). *Organizational transitions: Managing complex change*. Reading, MA: Addison-Wesley.

Beckhard, R., and Harris, R. (1987). *Organizational transitions*. Reading, MA: Addison-Wesley.

Bion, W. R. (1961). *Experiences in groups*. New York: Basic Books.

Bohm, D. (1990). *On dialogue*. Ojai, CA: David Bohm Seminars.

Bunker, B. B., and Alban, B. T. (Eds.). (1992). Large group interventions [Special Issue]. *Journal of Applied Behavioral Science, 28*(4).

Buzan, T. (1976). *Use both sides of your brain*. New York: Dutton.

Cabana, S. (1995a). Can people restructure their own work? *Target, 11*(6), 16–30.

Cabana, S. (1995b). Participative Design works, partially participative doesn't. *Journal for Quality and Participation, 18*(1), 10–19.

Dannemiller, K., and Jacobs, R. W. (1992). Changing the way organizations change: A revolution in common sense. *Journal of Applied Behavioral Science, 28*, 480–498.

Deming, W. E. (1992). *Quality, productivity, and competitive position*. Cambridge, MA: MIT Center for Advanced Engineering.

Deutsch, C. (1994, June 5). Round-table meetings with no agendas, no tables. *The New York Times*.

Emery, F. E. (1959). *The emergence of a new paradigm of work*. Canberra, Australia: Australian National University, Centre for Continuing Education.

Emery, F. E. (1995). Participative Design: Effective, flexible and successful, now! *Journal for Quality and Participation, 18*(1), 6–9.

Emery, F. E., and Emery, M. (1989). Participative Design: Work and community life. In M. Emery (Ed.), *Participative Design for participative democracy* (pp. 94–113). Canberra, Australia: Australian National University, Centre for Continuing Education.

Emery, F. E., and Trist, E. L. (1960). Socio-Technical Systems. In C. W. Churchman and others (Eds.), *Management sciences, models, and techniques*. London: Pergamon.

Emery, M. (Ed.). (1993). *Participative Design for participative democracy*. Canberra, Australia: Australian National University, Centre for Continuing Education.

Emery, M., and Purser, R. E. (1996). *The Search Conference: Theory and practice*. San Francisco: Jossey-Bass.

Fritz, R. (1989). *The path of least resistance*. New York: Fawcett Columbine.

Glidewell, J. C. (1970). *Choice points*. Cambridge, MA: MIT Press.

Hammer, M., and Champy, J. (1993). *Reengineering the corporation: A manifesto for business revolution*. New York: Harper Business.

Huntington, H. (1995). Open Space: An organization transition methodology (pp. 83–95). In H. Owen (Ed.), *Tales from Open Space*. Potomac, MD: Abbott.

Jacobs, R. W. (1994). *Real Time Strategic Change*. San Francisco: Berrett-Koehler.

Jayaram. (1977). Open systems planning. In T. Cummings and S. Srivastra (Eds.), *Management at work: A Socio-Technical Systems approach*. San Diego, CA: Pfeiffer.

Katz, D. T., and Kahn, R. L. (1978). *The social psychology of organizations*. New York: Wiley.

Kepferle, L., and Main, K. (1995). The University of Kentucky Center for Rural Health (pp. 39–43). In H. Owen (Ed.), *Tales from Open Space*. Potomac, MD: Abbott.

Klein, D. (1992). Simu-Real: A simulation approach to organizational change. *Journal of Applied Behavioral Science, 28*(4), 566–578.

Latane, B., and Darley, J. M. (1976). *Help in a crisis: Bystander response to an emergency*. Morristown, NJ: General Learning Press.

Le Bon, G. (1896). *The crowd: A study of the popular mind*. London: T. Fisher Unwin.

Lewin, K. (1943). Forces behind food habits and methods of change. *Bulletin of the National Research Council, 108*, 35–65.

Lewin, K. (1951). *Field theory in social science*. New York: HarperCollins.

Lippitt, R. (1980). *Choosing the future you prefer*. Washington, DC: Development Publishers.

Lippitt, R. (1983). Future before you plan. In R. A. Ritvo and A. G. Sargent (Eds.), *The NTL managers' handbook*. Arlington, VA: NTL Institute.

Main, T. (1975). Some psychodynamics of large groups. In L. Kreeger (Ed.), *The large group: Dynamics and therapy*. London: Constable.

Marrow, A. J. (1969). *The practical theorist*. New York: Basic Books.

Menzies, I.E.P. (1960). The functioning of social systems as a defense against anxiety. *Human Relations, 13*, 95–121.

Miller, E. J. (1986). Making room for individual autonomy. In S. Srivastva and Associates, *Executive Power: How executives influence people and organizations* (pp. 257–288). San Francisco: Jossey-Bass.

Miller, E. J., and Rice, A. K. (1967). *Systems of organization: The control of task and sentient boundaries*. London: Tavistock Institute.

Oshry, B. (1996). *Seeing systems*. San Francisco: Berrett-Koehler.

Owen, H. (1992). *Open Space Technology: A user's guide*. Potomac, MD: Abbott.

Owen, H. (1995). *Tales from Open Space*. Potomac, MD: Abbott.

Pasmore, W. A. (1994). *Creating strategic change: Designing the flexible, high performing organization*. New York: Wiley.

Public Broadcasting Service. (1994). *Challenge to America: The culture of commerce* (video).

Rehm, R. (1996). *Participative Design*. Unpublished manuscript.

Schindler-Rainman, E., and Lippitt, R. (1980). *Building the collaborative community: Mobilizing citizens for action*. Riverside, CA: University of California Extension.

Scott, J. F., and Lynton, R. T. (1952). *Three studies in management*. New York: Routledge.

Senge, P. M. (1990). *The fifth discipline: The art and practice of the learning organization*. New York: Doubleday.

Spencer, L. J. (1989). *Winning through participation*. Dubuque, IA: Kendall/Hunt.

Tichy, N. M., and Sherman, S. (1993). *Control your destiny or someone else will*. New York: Doubleday.

Trist, E. L., and Emery, F. E. (1960). *Report on the Barford Course for Bristol/Siddeley, July 10–16, 1960* (Tavistock Document No. 598). London: Tavistock Institute.

Trist, E. L., Higgin, G. W., Murray, H., and Pollock, A. B. (1963). *Organizational choice: Capabilities of groups at the coal face under changing technologies*. London: Tavistock.

Troxel, J. P. (1993). *Participation works: Business cases from around the world*. Alexandria, VA: Miles River Press.

Turquet, P. (1975). Threats to identity in the large group. In L. Kreeger (Ed.), *The large group: Dynamics and therapy*. London: Constable.

von Bertalanffy, L. (1950). *General systems theory*. New York: Braziller.

Weisbord, M. R. (1987). *Productive workplaces: Organizing and managing for dignity, meaning, and community*. San Francisco: Jossey-Bass.

Weisbord, M. R. (1992). *Discovering common ground*. San Francisco: Berrett-Koehler.

Weisbord, M. R., and Janoff, S. (1995). *Future Search*. San Francisco: Berrett-Koehler.

Wheatley, M. J. (1993). *Leadership and the new science: Learning about organization from an orderly universe*. San Francisco: Berrett-Koehler.

Zimbardo, P. G. (1970). The human choice: Individuation, reason, and order versus deindividuation, impulse, and chaos. In W. J. Arnold and D. Levine (Eds.), *Nebraska Symposium on Motivation*. Lincoln: University of Nebraska Press.

Index